IN THE
DRIVER'S SEAT
LOVE, LOSS AND LIVING WITH NO REGRETS

ALICIA ALLAIN SCHNEIDER
JOHN SCHNEIDER

for all those fighting the good fight

and trying to hold on

DISCLAIMER

The information presented is the authors' opinion and does not constitute any health or medical advice. The content of this book is for informational purposes only and is not intended to diagnose, treat, cure, or prevent any condition or disease. The statements made about products and services have not been evaluated by the U.S. Food and Drug Administration. Please consult with your own physician or healthcare specialist regarding the suggestions and recommendations made in this book.

Although the publisher and author have made every effort to ensure that the information in this book was correct at press time and while this publication is designed to provide accurate information in regard to the subject matter covered, the publisher and author assume no responsibility for errors, inaccuracies, omissions, or any other inconsistencies herein and hereby disclaim any liability to any party for any loss, damage, or disruption caused by errors or omissions, whether such errors or omissions result from negligence, accident, or any other cause.

Names have been changed where appropriate to protect identities and confidential materials. Any resemblance to actual persons, living or dead, or actual events is purely coincidental.

TABLE OF CONTENTS

Introduction 9

Round I: Trust.. **11**

Chapter One: There's No Way 13

Chapter Two: Why Now? 19

Chapter Three: House on Fire 25

Chapter Four: Life Moves On 31

Chapter Five: I Hate Cancer.. 35

Chapter Six: To Hell with Cancer... 40

Round II: Back in the Fire.. **47**

Chapter Seven: Black Ice 49

Chapter Eight: High Stakes... 57

Chapter Nine: The Machine 68

Chapter Ten: Just Keep Going 74

Chapter Eleven: Get Up 80

Chapter Twelve: Blazing Trails 84

Chapter Thirteen: Stay in the Fight 88

Chapter Fourteen: The Lifeboat 93

Chapter Fifteen: Moving On.. 98

Round III: Redefining Victory **103**

The Takeaways 117

Acknowledgments 119

One Last Thing.. 121

INTRODUCTION

"If you are not your own doctor,
you are a fool." – Hippocrates

Alicia Allain Schneider

Maybe you are reading this book because you've recently been diagnosed with cancer. Or maybe your loved one just got the terrible news. I've been there. One day I received that breaking news bulletin too and just like you, it was terrifying and confusing and I could not believe it was really happening to me.

So, if you just found out – scream, cry, curse, throw your phone at the wall, beat the steering wheel with your fist. Don't let anybody make you feel like you're not allowed to do those things. When you are ready, come back. I'll tell you my story and a few things I've learned that might help you along the way.

We were working on John's first memoir when I was diagnosed with stage four breast cancer. Our lives turned upside down, but as I was thrown into my own health crisis, I kept connecting with others who needed support and guidance until eventually, I felt the best thing I could do was write my own book to put in people's hands. When we go through something traumatic, one of the best ways to move forward is by helping someone else along. John and I truly believe that's why God brings us through.

You can make it through this. And you'll help others who are walking the path too.

John Schneider

In 1981, I recorded a song for the *Dukes of Hazzard* soundtrack album called "In the Driver's Seat." The lyrics talked about racing cars down a backroad and outrunning the law, but it was really a testimony about living by your own convictions and taking charge of your life, not just being a blind follower or going with the crowd. When I met this stunning woman from South Louisiana, that was one of the qualities I admired most about her. She was a go-getter, take charge, full of spit and fire, never content to sit by and let life just happen. It's a principal we share, a viewpoint that bonds us and guides everything we do.

That spirit has never been tested like this. At every turn, there's been temptations and tests trying to get us to give up the wheel and get out of the driver's seat. But that's not our way. Never has been, never will.

So, you'll hear my voice now and then because Alicia and I have walked through this trial side by side. We can't guarantee you'll win every battle by following this book and I won't promise that what you are about to read will "make your cancer dog 'sit'," as Alicia would say. But we hope the words, thoughts, prayers and memories between these covers will help you be in charge of the fight and perhaps more importantly, in charge of your life, to live one of strength, purpose, love and generosity.

ROUND I: TRUST

CHAPTER ONE
THERE'S NO WAY

April 2019

It was a perfect spring day in Holden, Louisiana, a tiny town an hour west of New Orleans and I had ten thousand people gathered in my backyard to watch my amazing boyfriend jump an orange Dodge Charger over a Livingston Parish police car. It would be the first time John "Bo Duke" Schneider *really* jumped the General Lee – not a stuntman– and fans from all over the country came to the second annual Bo's Extravaganza to watch him take flight.

Thank God they did because we needed it. John and I had been inseparable since I hired him to do a film I was producing a couple of years before and since that time, we'd weathered more than our share of severe storms. Our film studio flooded twice, wiping out everything we'd worked so hard to build. John was going through an ugly divorce and the financial fallout had already forced him to file bankruptcy and sell off all his memorabilia. He even spent a few days in the Los Angeles County jail.

Now, things were finally looking up. We had been working endless days from dawn until long after dark to bounce back, making new music, going on tour, and shooting films that we wrote and produced ourselves. Our latest project, a *Dukes of Hazzard* tribute, was set to start filming soon, and John's General Lee jump would be the first stunt captured for the movie.

The forecast had called for rain, which would have been a disaster for our event. I'm a high-strung person anyway, so the threat of storms plus John's stunt had me praying for help big time. The morning of the Extravaganza, the clouds parted, and the sun came through. Soon enough, the Ferris wheel was turning and bands started tuning up as thousands streamed through the gates. And when it was time for the main event, John floored it and shot the world's most famous car up and over the police car, landing safely in a pile of tires on the other side.

I ran to meet him at the General Lee, clinging to him, thanking God he was safe. As we stood arm in arm, waving to the cheering crowd, I thought,

He made it. We both did.

Little did I know, the worst storm was yet to come.

One month later...

I was being treated for a botched breast augmentation that had been giving me nightmares for years. A cosmetic surgeon in south Louisiana left my chest in a knotted mess of scar tissue that required a steady regimen of cortisone shots to manage the discomfort and pain. I was in for an exam with a new plastic surgeon to hopefully fix the damage when he noticed deep bruising and odd-looking strands on the surface of my skin.

"Hmm," he said, furrowing his brow. "I think you need to get this looked at right away."

I made a quick appointment with a local dermatologist in south Louisiana. They performed a biopsy the week before Memorial Day 2019 and scheduled an appointment to go over the results the following Monday. Soon after the initial biopsy, the dermatologist's office began calling me multiple times.

I didn't give it much thought. Our lives move a hundred miles per hour, all day, every day, and I'm constantly juggling multiple appointments and a packed itinerary. I figured the dermatologist just needed to reschedule my follow-up appointment, so I didn't return their call. Besides, John and I were set to start principal photography of our movie, *Christmas Cars*, that same Monday. I thought a little extra time could be a good thing.

But the doctor's office kept calling. Finally, I answered.

"Alicia, we need you to come into the office," the nurse said.

"Can this wait a couple of weeks?" I asked. "We're just about to start shooting a movie."

"No ma'am," she replied. "You have to come in today."

I paused, head spinning, trying to figure out what was going on. *When a doctor's office insists that you come in, it can't be a good thing, right? There's already too much craziness going on right now. I don't have time for this. They're probably just being overcautious.*

"Alright," I told the nurse. "I'll figured out a way to get over there today."

I ended the call and turned to John. He could tell by my face that something wasn't right. "I'm sure this is something about all the scar tissue in my breast," I told him. "I already know I've got issues. I'm gonna be in and out of there, quick."

I sped over and hustled into the office, still on the phone, trying to sort out shots and schedule for the film crew. My call ended quickly when the nurse spotted me and rushed me into the back. It's unusual to skip a doctor's office waiting room but I thought maybe, for once, they realized how busy I was and were trying to help me get in and out and back to work.

The dermatologist was waiting for me. I sat in the stiff plastic chair, still clueless. With a straight, no-nonsense tone, she dropped the bomb. "You have HER2 negative hormone receptor positive breast cancer and it may have spread to your bones and skin."

I sat confused, unable to speak or process the weight of her words.

"What?" I finally replied.

"We need you to get a mammogram and a sonogram," the doctor continued.

"Okay, sure," I replied, still thinking about the movie shoot and the busy days ahead. "I'll see if I can get that scheduled that in a week or two."

"No," she said. "You have to do this *now*."

I walked out to my car and headed back to the studio in a daze, still trying to process the dermatologist's report. It had to be a mistake. There was no way what she was saying could be accurate. We had already started production and a lot was riding on our film. Whatever it was, could wait.

My cell rang. It was the imaging center saying I had to come in for the mammogram. *Now.*

I hung up and called John. "The dermatologist thinks something might be wrong." I told him, "She wants me to get a mammogram and sonogram."

John

There's little pink building on our studio property that I use as my office and edit bay, and I was there preparing for the shoot. When Alicia called, I walked outside so as not to disturb the crew. Christmas movies are usually shot in the summer, but you have to wear winter clothes, of course, or it won't look much like the holidays. It was ninety degrees and humid that morning in south Louisiana. I was standing in the grass alone, wearing a wool coat and flannel shirt. That's when she told me that the doctor was sending her for more tests.

Alicia

"What?" John said. "Now? Today?"

"Right now," I said.

"Okay," John replied. "You go. I'll handle the shoot."

I hung up, turned the car around and headed up I-12, troubled thoughts spinning through my mind. *Cancer? There's **no** way. I'm healthy. It has to be a mistake. The medical industry makes these kinds of mistakes all the time. I'll go through these steps and take the tests, but I know what the outcome is going to be. I don't have time for this. I'm fine.*

I drove back to Baton Rouge and walked into the mammogram area of the imaging center. There were other women in the waiting room, most pale and gaunt, some with caps covering their bald heads. At that point, I wasn't even scared. It all just seemed so bizarre.

From the mammogram, they sent me straight into sonogram. "It's just scar tissue," I tried to explain. "I've had five surgeries just on this one breast to try and fix a bad procedure."

Medical procedures can be so dehumanizing. Take off your clothes, put on the paper gown, now wait in this other room with the other naked women, clutching your gown with your grippy hospital socks falling around your ankles. Stand still, lay flat, smash your breasts on the cold glass, down the hallway to another dark room and then you wait again.

Once they were done, I got dressed and drove back to the studio. John was shooting a scene from *Christmas Cars*, the one where his character, "Uncle Denver," is mourning at the gravesite of his deceased wife, Maudine. In the movie, John is singing our song, "Thank God You Do."

I don't know what you see in me / makes you want to see this through
but thank God you do / Thank God you do

I walked up quietly as John was strumming his guitar and singing along with the track. Not wanting to interrupt the scene, I stood there, watching as my not-yet husband sang a love song to his departed spouse while I carried the news that I had been branded with the scarlet letter – the Big **C**. It seemed like a strange twist of fate, like too much foreshadowing of events to come.

Tears streamed down my face as John's character talked about how lonely life had become without her love, how much he missed her in the small, sweet day-to-day moments. I struggled to hold it all together as the crew of eight worked to capture the footage for our film. Much of "Uncle Denver" and *Christmas Cars* was based on John's true-life story. Would this part come true too?

Was this God's way of showing me what my outcome would be?

Why?

We had both been through such a long and aimless season of life. John was going through a messy divorce that left him bankrupt, bitter, and possibly facing incarceration. I was a single mom struggling to find my way and life had become so difficult that honestly, there were moments when I prayed for God to take me home.

But then, I hired John to do my first film back in Louisiana and together we found better days. We were more than a couple; we were a team. "TTB. The team to beat," we laughed, and from the moment we met, we were nearly inseparable, making music, making films, traveling across the country doing shows and meeting the fans.

After a lot of difficult years, things were finally good. Better than good. They were perfect. There's a Bible verse that says, "I have found the one my soul loves." Finally, I'd found my soulmate.

John

After Alicia and I met, my mother said, "It's great to see that my son has his smile back." That's when I started calling Alicia "My Smile." We are soulmates. Anyone can see it and feel it. We feel it too.

Alicia

If God so obviously put us together, then why this? And why now?

I held all my confusion and pain inside until the shooting was done and the crew had gone home. My back porch looks out over the river and the trees and it's very dark there once the sun goes down. With the night sounds all around us, we sat in the side-by-side rocking chairs. Then, I reached over, took John's hand, and told him the news.

CHAPTER TWO
WHY NOW?

John

I've always had this odd sense that my writing could somehow see into the future. I preached the importance of taking charge of your life and it was more than simply a cinematic "device" that touched people's emotions.

When she broke the news to me that day, I could see the story that lay ahead, almost like the scenes of a movie, one that had a strong message and a good ending. "Okay, we'll fight this together," I told her. "I'll let the crew know and we'll finish this movie some other time."

"No, you will <u>not</u>," Alicia shot back, leveling me with a look that said she meant business. "We started this film and we're going to finish it. We are broke and need a hit for Christmas."

Alicia didn't put our work and dreams ahead of her health, but she was a realist in every sense of the word. And as a veteran of the business, a firm believer that the show must go on. We did need a hit. Something that would pull us out of the hole after a long season of financial disasters.

Anyone else would have buried their head in the sand, but not Alicia. You suck it up and keep going. We approached everything in life with that attitude and it's one of the many reasons we fell so hard for each other.

Alicia

My first night after the diagnosis was filled with anxiety. I already have OCD and attention-deficit tendencies and the thought of a malignant tumor attacking my body ramped up every anxious thought up to a whole new level. Denial, anger, depression – all those early stages of grief cycling through me over and over again.

Why would God do this to John and me just when we were getting our lives in order? He seemed to be blessing us and opening doors in every other area, so what glory or purpose could he possibly get out of something like this? *Why, God?* I cried out, tears streaming down my face again. *Why are you answering my prayer to take me home now?*

Then, I would try to deny it again, coming up with all the reasons the doctor's diagnosis could not be real. Labs make mistakes. The medical industry is so flawed. People get scary diagnoses all the time and it turns out to be some error in the system. Finally, I wore myself out and fell into a fitful sleep.

The next day, I told my parents and my daughter, Jessica, that I would have to undergo some medical tests. Otherwise, John and I decided to keep any news about cancer a secret.

Besides, we still had a film to make.

John

I reconfigured the schedule so we could continue to shoot *Christmas Cars* while going to all of Alicia's appointments. When you get a cancer diagnosis, your life becomes a nonstop barrage of doctor visits and tests. But we both love to work and it helped to keep our minds occupied and from worrying about the worst.

Alicia

The dermatologist's office made me an appointment for a consultation with an oncologist who specialized in treating breast cancers. After that, there were more biopsies on both breasts, lymph nodes, my spine. Though I have a high tolerance for pain, each time they extracted a sample of my tissue was insanely painful. Then, of course, there were more appointments, follow-ups, tests, exams, and consultations. Everything was accelerating now that I was thrust into the cancer treatment system, but John was by my side at all the appointments from there on.

The result of the biopsies on my breasts and lymph nodes confirmed a diagnosis of stage four HER2 negative hormone receptor positive cancer. It began to look like the writing was on the wall, so I called my daughter to come over. This sort of news is better told face to face.

While I was waiting, I thought about how I took care of cancer patients at my hair salon, ever since Jessica was about six months old. In 1996, I had left the motion picture business in Los Angeles and returned to Louisiana to style hair. A friend of mine was diagnosed with an aggressive brain cancer. She had beautiful long, brown hair at the time and I happened to know Renate Leuschner, a Hollywood wigmaker who had worked with Oliver Stone, Martin Scorsese, Tim Burton, Steven Spielberg and her most famous client – Cher. (She'd even worked with John on James Michner's film, *Texas*.)

"I know the best wigmaker in the world," I told my friend. "Why don't you let me get her to make something for you?"

Word got out and cancer patients began coming to me for help with their appearance. We would play around with wigs and different hairstyles, stenciling eyebrows, changing the makeup, just trying to bring some small point of joy and dignity to a brutal, demeaning experience. Women were going through such a horrible ordeal with the chemo and radiation and I wanted to help them feel pretty and loved and still have a feminine quality to their lives. Fighting the disease was hard enough, so I always felt called to give my time and services for free.

I had watched so many women suffer through treatment. Hundreds, even. Now, I had been diagnosed with stage four cancer. Would I need someone to help me?

I knew how the story usually ended. Most of the women that I worked with did not survive. The treatment seemed every bit as deadly as the disease. So why jump through all these hoops and go through all this pain and expense? What could I honestly hope for?

Jessica pulled into the driveway. I took a deep breath and tried to stop my hands from shaking. My daughter was the product of a show business marriage. Her father was a typical Hollywood agent, Italian suits and big cigars, struggling with addiction and adult responsibility. It broke my heart to know that her childhood had not been as stable as I'd hoped. And yet, she's the sweetest person, full of joy and hope and love for God and helping others.

I tried to be strong, but soon as Jess came through the door, I threw my arms around her and started bawling. "I just want you to know that I love you," I said through choking sobs. "Wherever the path leads us . . . I want you to know that I always fought for you. I made a lot of mistakes, baby. I know I did. I wasn't always as good of a mother as I wanted to be, and I didn't communicate like I should. But I have always loved you and wanted the best for you."

"Oh God, Mama," Jessica replied, tears brimming. "What's wrong?"

I held her close, told her the diagnosis and we both broke down again.

"Just know that wherever this journey takes us, I will always be with you," I promised. "Even if I am physically weak, even if I can't even speak."

A cancer diagnosis changes things. So many things we think are important aren't so important anymore. Perspective comes at a great price. You just want to say "I love you" over and over again to those you love. I was determined not to hide or shrink back. I didn't want my daughter to ever feel abandoned again.

John

After all the tears and thoughts of doom, Alicia had a supernatural calm that was truly heroic.

"The only way I can fight this is the same way we've fought everything else," she told me late one night. "Together. By our own convictions, in our own way. Anything else and we have already lost."

Alicia

I continued to meet regularly with my oncologist, Dr. Z. She offered encouragement, telling me that I would not necessarily have to lose my breasts. The FDA had recently approved a new medication called Ibrance that would enable me to prolong my life anywhere from ten to twenty years – but I would have to be on the medication for the rest of my life and the side effects were harsh.

"I've never been a big believer in taking medicine," I told her. "My grandfather believed that food is our medicine and that's the way that I have lived and kept myself in such good health to this point."

Don't get me wrong, my doctors were smart, strong, wonderful women. But I am a very hardheaded individual and I was not interested in getting on a ton of experimental medications, nor was I interested in getting sucked into the big cancer machine and letting it ruin the quality of whatever life I had left.

A few years back, a close member of my family was diagnosed with stage four cancer and given a short time to live. He refused chemo and radiation and was able to extend his life by several years through natural remedies. I would rather have less time and more quality than twenty years of fear, panic and feeling like hell.

But this was not the flu or shingles that I was fighting, and it is just so hard to figure out the right thing to do. I went back and forth over my options. I prayed a lot. I studied a lot. John and I talked and prayed about it all the time.

Meanwhile, the cancer machine kept pulling me into its gears. Biopsy, CT scan, sonogram, mammogram, MRI, ultrasound – and the next big step in diagnosis is the PET scan, an imaging test where they inject radioactive sugar through your veins and make you lie very still on a table while a camera takes 3D pictures of your internal organs.

The next morning, John and I met with my oncologist to go over the results. An image of my insides appeared, white spots littering the screen.

"The cancer has metastasized," Dr. Z said. "Your body is lit up like a Christmas tree. We need you to start on the Ibrance right away."

CHAPTER THREE
HOUSE ON FIRE

John

A little backstory first. I had just done a golf tournament to raise funds and awareness for ovarian cancer and through that network, Alicia and I met the UCLA oncologist who developed two ground-breaking cancer drugs, Herceptin and Ibrance, Dr. Dennis Slamon. Soon as Dr. Z suggested starting the meds, we were able to get directly in touch with him concerning Alicia's condition.

Alicia

Ibrance is a relatively new medication. It's not chemotherapy, but an aromatase inhibitor that slows the growth of cancer cells. I read over the long list of side effects: fatigue, anemia, nausea, diarrhea, respiratory infection, headaches, pulmonary embolisms. The studies showed that it extended the life span of most patients by about three years and cost nearly ten thousand dollars a month. Also, it would be a long process to get my insurance to approve, or even get the medication in stock.

Oh, well, so much for that then, I thought. *See ya. I'm outta here.*

But John got Dr. Slamon on the phone and he talked me down off the ledge a bit. "You're never going to be completely cured," Slamon told me. "But we can prolong your life and I am willing to help."

"Is there anything I can do on my own?" I asked.

"Go out in the sun wearing as little clothing as you can get away with," he advised. "Vitamin D3 helps fight cancer. You'll get more in twenty minutes wearing a tank top on a sunny day than you would taking a boxcar full of D3 supplements."

"I've got sixty acres back on the Tickfaw River," I replied. "I'll run naked through the swamp, if it'll help."

That's when I first began to see that treatment is a team effort, so the best thing I could do is build a strong team. I had Dr. Z and Slamon, but Z suggested I get a second opinion as well. She had done her fellowship at

Vanderbilt Hospital under a Polish oncologist named Dr. R. (*Due to HIPAA and the delicate nature of medicine, I'll refer to most of my physicians by the first letter of their name.*)

John and I worked in Nashville often and had a condo on Music Row. *Christmas Cars* had wrapped and we were making frequent trips to Tennessee at the time while making a gospel record and working on his first memoir with a local writer. The Vanderbilt campus was so close that we could see it from our building.

Dr. R agreed to take me on and I scheduled a consultation. She wanted to do bone samples, which required a spinal tap. If I thought the biopsies were painful....

"The tap will be able to tell one hundred percent what the diagnosis is," Dr. R assured us.

The first sample came back inconclusive. Dr. R went back in, studied the sample again and was able to verify that it was HER2 negative hormone receptor positive breast cancer. She started me on a hormone blocker until I was able to get the Ibrance. It would take about six weeks.

I was working all day on the album while helping edit the final cut of *Christmas Cars*, but still couldn't sleep, so at night I would frantically research my condition. There was plenty of information on HER2 positive, but not much on the negative. The only thing I knew was the doctors kept telling me that it was an aggressive disease. Even my plastic surgeon warned me. "Alicia," he said seriously, "don't play around with this."

I made the commitment to take Ibrance, but also began to investigate alternative treatments such as Gerson Therapy, which consists of coffee enemas and a steady stream of fresh, raw juice from vegetables and fruit. I spoke with a facility in San Diego that carried patients to a clinic in Mexico which specialized in therapies such as stem cell, oxygen, vitamin drips and hyperbaric chambers.

The amount of information out there is exhausting. But it's life or death so you must press on, through mounds of research and testimonials about everything from CBD to IV mistletoe and oil of oregano to wrapping yourself in tinfoil and doing yoga in a salt cave. When your house is on fire, you consider anything and everything that might put out the flames.

On a follow-up appointment at Vanderbilt, I asked my doctor, "What sort of adjunct therapies could I do to help the Ibrance work better?"

26

"Nothing," she replied.

"What do you mean, nothing?"

"The medication is sufficient," she said. "Let it do its work."

"How about clinical trials?" I asked. "Is there anything new out there that I could start adding in?"

"No, no," the doctor said. "This treatment plan has to fail first before we can refer you on to something like that."

That was unacceptable. The thought that there may be something better out there for me, but I could not access it until my current treatment plan "failed" made me crazy mad. How much worse off would I be by the time this treatment failed?

The industry will tell you that there is no other protocol. Your body can't fight cancer. You must move to the "passenger seat" and let the medical system fight for you.

Further research let me know that's how modern medicine works. Once you fail the mammogram, you can have a sonogram. If that fails, then you get a PET scan. And when you fail the PET scan, they tap your spine.

In my nighttime Googling, I came across an interesting term. "Standard of care" is what the medical industry has decided is the path and plan for the average patient. I didn't want average or standard treatment. I want *above* average. But "standard of care" means that when a person with a HER2 negative diagnosis comes in, this is path they are put on. It is not within the scope of practice to suggest juicing organic kale or taking sublingual full-spectrum CBD. Everybody who has diagnosis XYZ gets treatment ABC.

This was all a revelation to me. I was learning while trying to fight.

The lessons kept coming. Tests showed that I didn't have a genetic biomarker for the disease, but after my hysterectomy, I had been on hormone therapy, taking high doses of bio-identical, plant-based estrogen and testosterone. I learned many new terms at this time and one of the most important was "antigenesis" – which means any substance that causes your immune system to fight against it and create antibodies.

It can be a toxin, chemical, bacteria or virus. I felt that the trauma from five breast surgeries, coupled with high-dose hormones, had created an environment where cancer could thrive. The fact that the cancer wasn't hereditary made it more personal to me. If trauma and chemicals caused the tumors, then maybe I could change things and turn my health around.

The hormone blocker gave me immediate relief, which to me, confirmed my suspicions. But the Ibrance still cost a fortune and my insurance refused to cover treatment at Vanderbilt because it was out of state. If all of this sounds crazy, that's true to life because it *felt* crazy.

My life was a whirlwind before, managing John and running a company with multiple projects in the air. When you are self-employed, there are no sick days. If you don't work, the money stops coming in. A lot of people's income depended on my ability to hustle. I didn't have a safety net and I didn't have time to fight cancer. It was overwhelming.

Then, after you are overwhelmed and exhausted, the cancer machine picks up speed. You have to manage this as you become weaker and sicker by the day. I understood why people gave in and simply let the system take over the fight.

But I could never do things that way.

John

We were eating dinner with stuntman, Gary Baxley. Gary and I go way back. He was my stunt double on *Dukes of Hazzard*, coordinated stunts for *Christmas Cars*, and was on hand with fellow stuntman Jack Gill to help me finally jump the General Lee at Bo's Extravaganza in 2019.

We were discussing future projects. Gary didn't know about the diagnosis or what we were going through. Suddenly, he pointed to Alicia while staring me straight in the eye. "So, John," Gary said. "When are you two getting married?"

Stuntmen tend to be blunt. Alicia and I exchanged glances. "Do you want to get married?" I asked.

"I would love to marry you," my Smile replied.

Gary and I kept talking about the logistics of jumping a Dodge Hellcat over the river. After a while, I turned to Alicia. "Hey. Did we just get engaged?"

"Yeah," she said. "I think we did."

"Okay. When you want to get married?"

She put her fork down. "You got the calendar?" Alicia said.

I pulled our itinerary up on my phone and we scanned it over. "How 'bout July 2nd?" she asked.

"Okay," I agreed. "July the second it is." We sealed the deal with a quick kiss and got back to work.

That scene might sound a little cavalier, but getting engaged while planning a car stunt was totally our style, our life, our way. You know that part in the Bible that talks about a couple being equally yoked? That's us, completely.

CHAPTER FOUR
LIFE MOVES ON

So much was happening and so many thoughts were racing through my mind that I decided it might be helpful to start keeping a journal. I wanted to capture everything and have a place to let it all hang out, something I could pass on to my family or go back and learn from later.

One morning, not long after John and I got engaged, I put down these words.

June 19th, 2019

The strange thing is life just keeps moving on. A stage four diagnosis feels like the end of the world, but babies are still being born and people fall in love and go to work and pay bills and the earth keeps on turning. I guess that's what we mean when we say, "It is what it is."

Sooner or later, everybody faces their own mortality. I've always struggled with that, with my reasons for being here, for taking up space on this planet, knowing that eventually, we all die and most of the things we thought were so important will fade away.

The hardest thing is feeling like you are not being seen or heard and it's easy to slip into that frame of mind when you are being thrust deeper and deeper into the medical system. The process can be so impersonal. Last name, date of birth. Social security number. Here's your ID bracelet, wait in this room with all these other sick people and then go wait in another room by yourself. They stick you with needles and draw endless vials of blood, countless x-rays, scans, and tests, reducing you to a series of numbers and images on a screen. You become less of a person and more of a diagnosis.

To be honest, some days I've struggled with even wanting to be here anymore. Not so much to end my life – just like, stop this crazy Ferris wheel of sickness and uncertainty. I want to get off. If this is a game, it's not fun anymore. I'm getting my butt kicked. I want to quit and go home with God.

Then I sit before a doctor who's reading results of my biopsy and talking like I'm already dead, like there's not much hope at all. That will make you look at things in a different way. The process is a lot of up and down, hope and desperation, getting excited and being let down. That's exhausting in itself.

I want to live. I've got too much to do, too many people to help, adventures to experience, movies to make. John and I have so many dreams. That's where the drive comes from. You make your own hope. Stir up faith. Make a decision to fight. But it's not easy. You wake up with a new determination but by noon, you're ready to give up again.

None of this makes any sense to me. I don't have any genetic markers or history of cancer to worry about. My blood work is always great. I'm insurable! That says a lot right there.

It's okay to throw a little pity party. But after the party, you still have hard choices to make. My research says it's crucial to cut sugar. Makes sense to me. How do they light up tumors for a PET scan? By giving you a sugary drink. (Let me get this straight: The medical industry knows cancer cells suck up glucose to thrive – yet they won't suggest that patients cut back on sugar? What's that about?)

One I figured out that cancer loves sugar, I started by cutting it in all forms, cold turkey. That means no bread. How do you live in South Louisiana with no bread? No M&Ms at night, which is my favorite. No rice. No wine. No margaritas. A Cajun with no wine or beer? That's a huge part of our culture, a celebration of life and friends, letting the good times roll. Is that what they mean by the cure being worse than the disease?

John and I drank through the last disaster, the back-to-back floods that wrecked our studio and home. Sometimes you need something to take the edge off a rotten, terrible day. Help me, Jesus and a little tequila, amen. We got through those dark days. Now, there's trouble and struggle again. No tequila this time. "Help me, Jesus," again.

The doctors feel I'm about three years into this disease. I am optimistic, but will try to balance hope with reality, because studies show that the average survival rate for my diagnosis is about five years. If I can make it beyond that, the chances of survival improve. But if I'm already three years in and the clock is ticking…. I don't know if John realizes that.

Good thing is, whatever I set my mind to, I give it my all. I am relentless. Whether it's getting us back on our feet after the flood, getting through divorce and money problems, helping my parents, my daughter. Now it's time, to give this fight my all.

We fly out tomorrow to do bone biopsies. Then on to San Antonio, Houston and Nashville. I'll be in doctor's appointments while John records his first gospel album, *Recycling Grace*. He's doing an old spiritual called "Satan, Your Kingdom Must Coming Down." Amen to that and amen to recycling grace.

My biggest prayer through this trial is to have grace, to give it and receive it too, to let grace flow through every part of my life. To not take it all too seriously and forget to laugh. To love with all my heart, each moment, every minute, for as long as God gives me life.

Amen.

CHAPTER FIVE
I HATE CANCER

I was producing a movie, making records, putting together a band, battling cancer and traveling back and forth between Nashville and South Louisiana. Even with all that on my plate, don't believe I wasn't thrilled to be planning a wedding too. There was just one problem: John's divorce was dragging on in California with no end in sight.

In typical "team to beat" fashion, we determined that there were two kinds of wedding ceremonies. One for the state and one in the eyes of God. So, I called a dear pastor friend of mine back in my hometown and set up a meeting to plead our case. John and I sat in Pastor Tom's office spilling out our story, movies and soulmates and the state of California refusing to budge, floods and financial struggles, all the music we'd made and the stuff we had been through together. And in the middle of all these battles, an extremely difficult diagnosis. Would he agree to join us together in the eyes of God?

With a smile, Pastor Tom replied, "I think we can work something out."

The morning of our wedding, I got a text from my friend, Jana.

Hey, I need to come talk to you.

Jana runs cancer camps for children. She's a devoted Christian, with all the intuition and wisdom that comes to someone very close to God. I replied right away.

Sure. Come on by.

Jana walked in and looked around at all the decorations, garland and tiny lights, cakes and fancy napkins, a love seat with hand-painted signs on each side. John's sign said, "**Mr. Right**" while mine said "**Mrs. *Always Right*.**" (He loved those signs.)

"What's going on?" Jana asked.

"Oh," I replied. "I'm getting married today."

"Girl, why didn't you tell me?" she said. "I'll come back another time."

"Come on, Jana, sit down," I told her. "Obviously there's a reason why you reached out and I answered. Let's talk."

We sat by the big picture window in my kitchen. Jana paused, collected herself, then leaned in. "I have to tell you something," she said. "You are on the right path. People are going to try and move you off this path, but you already know the right thing to do."

After a long embrace and a few tears, Jana left me to my prepare for the ceremony. As she drove away, I gave thanks to God for a special wedding gift – confirmation that I was going the right way. It was exactly what I needed to slip out from under the dark cloud of cancer and become a silly, lovesick, hope-filled southern girl on the day that she marries the man of her dreams.

John

Family and friends filled the old barn on our studio grounds to watch Pastor Tom Shepard tie the knot. Alicia was radiant in a sleeveless cream-colored dress and I was doing my best to be dashing in a tan linen suit with a gold tie. She was and *is* the most beautiful bride I have ever seen.

Once the ceremony was complete, we moved the reception outside. Alicia and I toasted our union with champagne and stepped out for our first dance as husband and wife. Alicia loved to "pop" fireworks and loved to surprise me with them even more. As soon as the first downbeat of our song hit, a stream shot up and lit the skies above us with a shower of sparks. With everything else on her mind, she still made time to make our moment even more magical, just to see the look of wonder in my eyes.

When it was over, we climbed in that orange Dodge Charger and drove away with a big "JUST MARRIED" sign and tin cans tied to the back. It was a perfect day, the happiest I had been in a very, very long time.

Alicia

But the business never sleeps and since John and I work 25/8, we had to postpone our honeymoon and get back on the road. The tour bus was hard on my body, but by the grace of God, we were able to get a nice camper to travel in so I could rest while John performed.

John

It's forty-five feet long. That's a *motorhome* – NOT a camper!

Alicia

Whatever, it's a CAMPER. See, the whole time we're traveling, whether it's three miles or three thousand, we are picking and sparring with each other, cutting up. We may not have taken an official honeymoon, but when you're happy and in love it's all honeymoon, whether you're at the Eiffel Tower or the Love's Truck Stop just out of Smut Eye, Alabama.

Late one night, while John was driving, I stared out the window as the white lines passed by. *Okay, God,* I prayed. *I'm not going to beg you to save my life. I'm asking you to get me through this so I can help others. So, instead of "why now?" – I'm asking you to help me figure out "what now?" instead.*

I continued to research with every moment of down time and learned that the medical industry's position is that diet has nothing to do with cancer. According to their studies, there was nothing I could do to support the treatment, not with food or supplements or exercise.

There was no way I could sit by and wait to see if the medication would work for me. I was determined to be proactive. My mind was open to anything that might help me find a path to destroy the cancer cells and regain my health.

I spent about six weeks doing serious research into my diagnosis, checking out any suggestion, YouTube video or internet post about something that had helped someone beat HER2 negative hormone receptor positive breast cancer.

John and I talked with the Gerson Institute in Tijuana about going down for a two-week stay and met with a tall, odd-looking, white-gloved man in a North California cherry orchid who took a sample of my blood, smeared it on a piece of regular paper and studied the patterns. That seemed a little voodoo even for someone who grew up near New Orleans. Thanks, but no thanks. Gonna pass on that one.

There are so many options and strategies. Some are incredibly difficult and expensive. I was being pulled in different directions between alternative medicine (some seemingly legit and others downright wacky) and giving myself over to Vanderbilt and the cancer machine.

But the idea that kept coming back to me was to try and beat the tumors through vitamins, supplements and a focused diet. Could I really eat my way back to health? When there's so much at stake, it's hard to know the right thing to do.

When we returned from California, I got back to my studies with a new passion. My friend's message of confirmation had encouraged me to dig even deeper. I started by reading Miriam Kalamian's *Keto for Cancer* book which talks about how a low-carb ketogenic diet can cause cancer to begin to consume itself. The PET scan had shown me first-hand how sugar makes tumors light up. Cancer loves sugar. I hate cancer. So, I would starve cancer of what it loved and bombard my body with all the things that cancer hates.

Earlier, I had been speed-dating various treatments, rushing through the highlights of a book or video, but once I figured out my path, I dove in deep. I can be very OCD, but as a child, I learned to make those obsessive tendencies work for me instead of against, my friend instead of an enemy. I began to fanatically read everything I could about nutrition and cancer, researching my condition, various protocols of treatment, experimental approaches, natural therapies, and alternative treatment centers. I buried myself in books, videos, testimonies, and went down every rabbit hole the internet had to offer, from drinking your own urine (!!!) to injecting tumors with gold.

Cancer had knocked me down. But now it was time to make my plan to fight back.

CHAPTER SIX
TO HELL WITH CANCER

I spent the remainder of 2019 doing the standard of care at Vanderbilt while carefully building and tweaking my adjunct strategy. As time passed, I was able to dial in my keto diet, adding in certain fruits and vegetables, taking other things out and changing the amount of daily carbs depending on how I felt. John and I figured out how to make keto lasagna and zero sugar pecan pie, but we still both lost weight.

Keto drops weight *fast* and while most of us would love to lose a few pounds, I didn't want to look emaciated and sick. "What's the least you've ever weighed and felt good about yourself?" John asked.

At the time, I weighed one hundred and thirty-seven pounds and wanted to get back to a number that was closer to my younger days. "One-fourteen," I replied.

"Okay, we won't worry about it unless you get under that number," he said. "And if you do, we'll bump it back up. Regardless, we'll be the ones in control."

That gave us peace about the Keto, but there were plenty of other plans to put in place to assure we were doing everything possible to fight. Pretty much everything I read said to run the other way from any kind of artificial sweetener. I think tumors love aspartame even more than sugar. We switched to using monk fruit and stevia instead. I also threw out my deodorant (because of the aluminum) and toothpaste (fluoride) and anything that wasn't all-natural. (If your toothpaste carries a warning not to swallow, throw it out!)

I was taking so many vitamins and minerals every day that I probably rattled when I walked and put so much CBD oil under my tongue that John and I decided to start our own brand. Instead of CBD, we called it CBoD and made "Yee Haa" flavors like Apple Pie Moonshine. All these years later, the Dukes are back running shine. (the legal kind*)*

Asian countries use medicinal mushrooms in the treatment of certain cancers, so I added in a blend which included Maitake, Lion's Mane and

Turkey Tail to reduce inflammation and build my immune system. Each day I did cardio, either walking the loop on Music Row with John or on the treadmill if the weather was bad. I also used weights to get my heart rate up to a hundred and fifty beats per minute for twenty minutes at a time and did intense sessions in the infrared sauna at up to one hundred and fifty-eight degrees.

Cancer hates heat. Tumors wither when body temperature gets over one-hundred and four and I knew it was important to weaken cancer while strengthening my immune system. And I knew it was something I'd have to do every day.

Some studies showed that Panacure, a medication for dogs, could kill cancer cells. The research was far from conclusive, but it seemed safe, inexpensive and with a diagnosis like mine, I thought, *screw it, I'll try anything. What do I have to lose?*

John made a lot of jokes about me taking puppy dewormer and sometimes I'd play along by panting with my tongue out and lifting my leg. We've always picked at each other and had a lot of fun together and there's no way that I was going to let cancer take that away.

I set my mind and heart to go deeper spiritually too, imagining God's love and light from the top of my head to tip of my red toenails. Growing up Catholic, I said the Lord's Prayer every day. For a South Louisiana girl, praying "Our Father, who art in Heaven…" came as naturally as saying your ABCs, sometimes to the point of repetition where you don't give enough thought to the words.

After the diagnosis, I started really thinking about that prayer, especially the part that says, "thy will be done on earth as it is in Heaven." We are all God's creatures. He made us perfect. We're the ones who mess it up.

Spiritually, physically, emotionally – I started believing for God's will on earth, just like it is in Heaven. When it comes to religious beliefs, there are a lot of things up for debate, but God hates sickness and disease. You can't argue that. Jesus healed people everywhere he went, regardless of race, denomination or social status. So, I say the prayer much slower now and I think about the words.

John's memoir, *My Life, My Way*, (a nod to his song "In the Driver's Seat") came out in November of 2019, telling the behind-the-scenes stories of *Smokey & the Bandit*, *Dukes of Hazzard*, *Smallville* and John's chart-topping career in country music. He even has a chapter about moving in with Johnny Cash.

John

After *Dukes* wrapped, I lived with Johnny and June for about a year and half. When he didn't have to be "Johnny Cash," John R. had a real easy way of being and we'd just hang out fishing Old Hickory Lake and talking about the stuff in life that really matters. When I was a boy, I'd sit in my Grandma Dugan's living room, playing guitar and singing Johnny Cash songs. Then I grew up and my hero became one of my very best friends.

Johnny and June's marriage is legendary, but I got to see it up close, the way their hands would always reach for each other, the looks that would pass between them on even the most ordinary of days.

"I hope someday I can find my June," I'd tell John.

"Don't worry," he'd say with that rugged old smile and a rumble in his voice. "She'll find you." When John R. Cash told you something, you believed it.

It took nearly three decades, but she did. Many nights I would hold Alicia tight and tell her, "I finally found my June."

Alicia

Shortly after the memoir came out, we released *Christmas Cars*, John's tribute to Denver Pyle, Hazzard and his trusted stallion, the General Lee. We were promoting the film in Nashville when I received an early Christmas gift.

My PET scan showed a significant decrease in cancerous activity, from lit up like a Christmas tree to one tiny yellow spot off the bone. Doctors were astounded by my progress. The treatment plan was working. My house was still on fire, but the flames were dying, more and more, with each passing day.

The ground beneath me felt more stable and I wanted to find ways to help others facing this disease and pass on the things I'd learned. We started by making the rounds to various media outlets to share about my battle with breast cancer. Prayers were answered and hardly a day passed that someone didn't reach out to talk about what they were going through.

Team Schneider kept trucking along into the new year, playing shows and making appearances. After the success of *Christmas Cars*, John wanted to give a nod to his old friends Burt Reynolds and Jerry Reed with his own twist on the legend of the Bandit and Snowman. We started filming *Stand on It!* early that year with lots of wild stunts and car chases and it felt like our life was beginning to get back to normal.

At this point, I was doing scans every few months to keep an eye on things. Early that spring, I met with Dr. Z to go over my latest PET. John and I studied the images on the screen. No lit-up markers, no spots of any kind. I wanted to be certain of what I was really seeing.

"It's clear?" I asked.

"Your scan is totally clear," Dr. Z confirmed. "You turned it around." She shook her head, smiling. "When my kids are older, I am going to study everything you did."

Less than a year after the original diagnosis of stage four breast cancer, my scans showed zero signs of activity. John and I were over the moon as we celebrated with champagne and prayers of gratitude. In every milestone, I've always offered gratitude. It was a good day, a good night and we were living a good life.

Even though we were having a tough time, many had it far worse and we didn't feel like it was the time to pull back on helping others. We did a lot of outreach in that season, and thank God, neither of us got sick. Hospitals were struggling under the weight of the pandemic, so John invited Kix Brooks and Kellie Pickler for an online benefit concert to help Children's Miracle Network.

John

I was an overweight kid with asthma and my mom often had to bring me in for testing to those big, scary hospitals with their dingy waiting rooms and sick adults coughing and wheezing, parked out and waiting to die in the hall. It was a terrible experience and I swore that someday, when I was able, I would do something so other kids wouldn't have to go through that. Together with a few like-minded friends, I co-founded Children's Miracle Network and in forty years, we've raised just over eight billion dollars for children's hospitals.

Miracles seldom happen on their own. They need our help, our prayers and our sweat equity. I've been at it since I was sixteen. Sometimes, I get

ALICIA ALLAIN AND JOHN SCHNEIDER

tired and my doctor suggests that maybe it's time to slow down. I have always had a passion to help the less fortunate and after what Alicia and I are going through, I want to find ways to help those struggling with this awful disease. To hell with cancer. Send it back where it belongs.

Alicia

With *Stand on It!* ready for release, I put together a fun tour of drive-in theaters, screening a double feature with *Christmas Cars*. Sometimes John and his band would play a concert as well, if the venue had the capabilities. I was off the oncology meds but tried to stay on my adjunct program to keep my body strong and any rouge cancer cells at bay. Finding an infrared sauna isn't easy when you are on the road, especially in a pandemic. The world was crazy, life was hectic and there were times when I let things slide.

John was shooting a Christmas movie in Nashville with Reba McEntire when the deadliest flash flood to ever hit the Volunteer State devastated Middle Tennessee. We loaded up an eighteen-wheeler and headed to Humphreys County to hand out food, water, clothes, diapers and toys.

Everybody was soaking wet and exhausted. It's hard to be careful in that kind of crisis, but we also gave out a whole lot of hugs, handshakes and prayers for blessing and help to make it through. Even though the Covid alarms were still going off 24/7, neither of us caught the virus.

Not ten days later, while John and I were still helping with flood relief, Hurricane Ida stuck South Louisiana. Once again, our film studio was ravaged by the brute force of Mother Nature. A big tree fell and crushed the General Lee we'd used in *Christmas Cars* and destroyed John's mother's old house, Miss Shirley's, which we had been using as our store. Several other buildings flooded and a few roofs and big trees were lost to the wind.

Stand on It! was a much-needed smash and before the hurricane hit, we'd been buzzing around the studio filming scenes for the follow-up, *Poker Run*. In that movie, the race is on as the challenges get tougher and stakes higher than ever before. It proved to be a strange piece of foreshadowing. Another sequel was coming as life would imitate art once again.

ROUND II:
BACK IN THE FIRE

CHAPTER SEVEN
BLACK ICE

In the fall of 2021, John and I were asked to speak at The Truth About Cancer event held at the Gaylord Opryland Hotel in Nashville. I'd been looking for ways to give back and this was my chance. I gave my testimony, telling the sold-out crowd how God, prayer and staying in the driver's seat helped me become cancer-free in five months.

I also talked about the "old ways" and the importance of our roots. Our ancestors didn't have all the technological advantages that we have today. They had to lean on faith and the wisdom of the land. Thank God for technology and modern medicine, but I think we've forgotten some important things.

When I was a little girl, I could see my granddad's kitchen light from my bedroom window. Many nights, he would be sitting at the table, glasses on the end of his nose, eating raw garlic and reading some book. He was an eccentric little man, curly black hair and red suspenders over a pearl snap cowboy shirt, Dickies tucked into white shrimp boots, which we call "Cajun Reeboks."

Grandad was obsessed with learning, ordering various seeds and plants, studying the best ways for a person to live in divine health. My grandfather was eventually diagnosed with Alzheimer's and given eight years to live. Through his studies, he was able extend it another eight years beyond that.

One day, near the end, he took my hand and said, "Pumpkin, the key to life is your minerals." He taught me about the soil and the garden, the importance of natural foods and living close to the land. I'd gotten away from all that, so I wanted to remind myself as I reminded all the people in attendance that day. Look to the future, but don't forget the past.

After I finished speaking, John came out to sing "I Hate Cancer." Then we went into our silly-couple-teasing-each-other act and everybody laughed.

John

"Alicia and I were on the way over here in the MOTORHOME."

Alicia

"That thing we travel in is a *camper*. Ugh."

John

Actually, I sang two songs that day. And spoke a bit.

Alicia

My husband is a ham.

John

Well, I had some things I wanted to say.

Alicia

Right? You always do. Okay, this is my book. You had yours. Stay in your lane…

John

Hang on. I want to tell the reader the same thing I told the crowd at Opryland Hotel that day. How lucky and blessed I am to be married to the most remarkable person I have ever met and how proud I am of how she's handled herself through all of this.

Alicia never asked, "Why me?" The first thing she said after we got the diagnosis was, "I must be going through this for a reason. It has to be so I can help other people get through it too." That's been her attitude all the way through. I've seen her exhausted and in pain and she will still make time to reach out and help others.

I might be "famous", but she's the star.

Alicia

Well, a lot of people reached out to help me along the way. We help each other. That's what we're supposed to do.

Anyway, I finished my speech by saying, "If anyone has questions or just wants to talk, I'll be at a booth in the foyer." When I got there, the line stretched around the corner and out of sight. I held back tears, finally seeing how all things could be working together for the good.

***

After a series of clear PET scans, I felt like the worst was behind me and I was ready for a break from the medical machine. My adjunct therapies seemed solid and effective and we were ready to get back to living our 100-mile-an-hour life.

Following the success of *Stand On It!* and *Poker Run,* John and I had been talking about making a racing movie together called *Winner Takes All,* the story of a man and a woman on the same racing team who have a rivalry on and off the track, fueled by a lot of ego, drive and attitude on both sides. As the season progresses, the feud builds, until finally, the two make a "winner takes all" bet for the racing season finale, in this case, the victor getting the loser's car.

In the film, my character slams into the wall during a race. The car explodes in flames and she narrowly escapes. Her back is broken and she's mentally and spiritually battered as well – but her spirit remains.

She fights back, step by step, battling the odds, battling the doctors who tell her she'll probably never walk again. By grit and faith, she returns for the final race, climbing back into her car for the showdown and . . . well, I won't give away the ending, but a lot of it is based on me and John's love story.

And sometimes, stories seem to influence real-life because crazy thing is, we started working on the *Winner Take All* storyline before I had the actual crash. I was eager to scratch that need for speed and adrenaline anyway, so John and I had started practicing laps on dirt tracks. I felt like Superwoman in that car, hitting the straightaways and banking the curves. Maybe in hindsight I should have been more respectful of the gift of healing God had given me, but I believe God gave us life to live to the fullest and when I put the hammer down in that race car, I felt more alive than I had in a long, long time.

John's been racing since he was a teen, doing donuts in his little white Triumph TR-6, hot-rodding the back roads of Georgia. He loved outlaw car runs so much that he skipped school and jumped the fence at the Lakewood Fairgrounds in Atlanta so he could sneak onto the set of *Smokey and the Bandit.*

John

In the final scene, as Buford chases Bandit's Cadillac, you'll see a tire roll towards a tall guy in a black cowboy hat and then the frame freezes and they roll the end credits. Yep, that's me. Sure, it's only a few seconds, but you know what they say, "When the legend outshines the truth … print the legend!"

Alicia

I did my share of drag racing too, as a teenage girl in South Louisiana, tearing down some dark country highway in my little red Fiero, T-tops open, wind in my hair, Information Society booming from the big bass speakers behind the seat. The "Serotonin Uptake Machine." That's what I called my car. It was always a good time in my ride.

Here's a quick story that'll give you some insight: I'm fourteen years old, still in my cheerleader outfit with the sheriff's daughter riding shotgun in my much-older boyfriend's Mercedes 190E. We're doing seventy in a forty-five, windows rattling because the music's so loud. Suddenly, blue lights fill my rearview mirror.

So, I pulled over quickly and started to apologize and cry. Right?

Nope. I stomped on the gas, leading police on a high-speed chase through the streets of my small southern town. It was like real-life *Dukes of Hazzard*. At some point, I might've even yelled "*YEE HAA!*" I would've outrun that Roscoe P. Coltrane too, but we got caught in traffic at the only bridge in town.

Cops surrounded the Benz with pistols drawn. I got out slowly, hands lifted, trying to keep my cheer skirt from riding up. The officer cuffed me and stuffed me in the back of his car. When they got me down to the station and called my daddy, he told them to "keep her little ass in jail!"

Didn't stop me though. Before long, I was out burning tires again. I'd gotten a taste of high-speed thrills and now it was in my blood. 280Z, Camaro, RX-7, Porsche Boxster flying down the PCH. Some beat cancer and go skydiving to feel alive again. I wanted to race cars.

We had plans for my character to drive a pink "Double D" stock car with the breast cancer ribbon on top and "I Hate Cancer" stenciled on the back. Our team had the die-cast model complete, but in the meantime, I was racing the black 00 "Stand On It" car. It was October of 2021 and John and

I were at the Pike County Speedway in Mississippi. I had a custom-made seat with a six-point harness in an open-wheeled modified outlaw stock car with no airbags and nothing between me and the engine but a firewall and sheet metal frame.

I hit the second turn and went into a spin, turning down towards the infield to let the other drivers pass on the high bank. An inexperienced driver sped into the turn and smashed into me head-on. I broke both axles on the car but shook it off and climbed out. Racing fans stood to applaud and offer support as the tow truck carted me off the field. The crash tweaked my back pretty good, but I didn't think much of it at the time, though now, looking back, I probably racked up the first spinal compression right there.

John and I spent Thanksgiving in Nashville with my daughter, Jessica, as she moved up to start a new job in the mental health field. My back was hurting but I've struggled with that pretty much all my life, so I didn't give it much thought.

Five days before Christmas, John and I took the cars out to a speedway in Ringgold, Georgia for some practice. He was driving the 01 Duke while I was in the double-zero "Stand On It" car again. We were the only ones on the track that day, keeping a good distance between us.

John

After Alicia's crash at Pike County, we were determined to get some "seat time" in at a friend's track. Well, my Smile's wreck wasn't the only reason. We'd been racing at speedways across the south as part of "Bo's Extravaganza: On the Road" and I was tired of coming in at the back of the pack. Not a good look for "Bo Duke."

We went to practice in Ringgold that day to be safer and better prepared for our next race. I remember roaring past the start/finish line, coming down the straightaway into turn one and having the rear of my car suddenly shift about a yard to the right.

That's no good, I thought, chickening out and easing through the first turn.

On the next lap, I slowed down to get a better look. Water was leaking onto the racetrack from the barrier wall, maybe from a busted pipe or a spring under the grandstand. I tried to find a better way around it, but on my third lap, the back half of the car started shaking and my rear differential shattered, spitting grease and metal pieces all over the track.

Alicia would have fought me over leaving, but I should've called it right then and there. We should have loaded the cars up and headed home.

Alicia

Once John got towed, I had the track to myself, so I went for it, full out. About lap fifteen I started feeling good, having fun, pushing the car harder with each new trip around the track. In addition to the slick spot before turn one, the packed dirt had started to dry out with blacktop showing through in places – known in racing as "black ice."

I was coming out of the first turn, eyeballing the straightaway for my next point of entry, pedal to the metal when I hit a patch of hardpack. The car's back end grabbed the surface and got out in front of me, sending me straight for the infield wall.

I hit the concrete center barrier at full speed, then the car spun sideways and crashed into the wall again. When I finally stopped spinning, my upper body was flung forward like I'd been mule kicked into the steering wheel and the car's engine had pierced the firewall and was sitting beside me. Time passes slow in trauma. I looked at the sputtering motor and the twisted steel around me. I tried to take a deep breath but couldn't. Reality set in quick and with it, a hard conviction.

God, I am so sorry, I prayed. *Let me walk out of this and I will never get in another race car as long as I live.*

Finally, I was able to draw a breath. I crawled out of the car as two track employees ran to help. "Just take care of the car," I told them as I staggered in a daze towards our camper. John and our mechanic looked at me when I walked in, not quite understanding what was going on. I moved past them and laid down on the bed, trying to gather myself.

John

When Alicia walked past me to the motorhome, I didn't know she was hurt. I thought maybe she was just done for the day.

I should have known something was wrong even if she didn't make a big deal out of it. There's something about racing that makes a driver more focused on their car than their own well-being. I should've taken Alicia to the ER immediately.

That moment haunts me. It will haunt me for the rest of my life.

Alicia

I laid there, hardly able to move. That's when I figured out that I was in deep trouble. My hips and legs were on fire and I could tell my back was seriously out of whack. I tried to reconstruct the crash, replaying the details in my mind.

If I'd been thrown forward, that means one of my restraints must have been loose. But just a little bit, a few inches, or else I wouldn't have survived the crash. Instead, my hips were locked down tight while my upper body got whiplashed by the impact into the wall. I thought about all the danger I'd come through in the last couple of years, the wars I'd fought, the scars inside and out. Anxiety gripped me, so I started to pray again.

By the grace of God, I did not end up in the emergency room. For whatever other struggles I have, I believe God heals and that he made our bodies to repair themselves. I've done that my whole life. I could write another book of testimonies of the times God and faith intervened and I walked away from what should have been serious injury, illness, or death. So, I felt sure I could keep fighting and walk away again.

Besides, it was Christmas, the season of miracles, and we wanted to go home.

CHAPTER EIGHT
HIGH STAKES

It sounds crazy, but after the crash at the racetrack, I didn't go to the doctor. There was just too much going on. We were trying to get back so we could celebrate Christmas with family and friends and there were so many distractions.

I thought I was probably just bruised up. John was hurting all over too, so we weren't sure if it was exhaustion or possibly even a Covid thing. I figured with a little time and rest back home in Louisiana, I would be just fine.

As the days passed, the pain in my back and legs became more intense. I would cry all through the night and each morning it would take thirty minutes before I could even put my feet on the ground. The doctor's office called in some hydrocodone, but it barely touched the pain.

My gut told me I should get in touch with my local oncologist, Dr. Z. It had been a few months since I'd had a complete checkup and I thought it might be smart to get a baseline since my body had been through such a shock. While waiting for insurance to approve my oncology visit, I went ahead and made an appointment with my internist. Older adults need more than just a general practitioner, so John and I see an internal medicine doctor, one who specializes in the prevention, diagnosis, and treatment of internal diseases. He ordered some standard tests.

"Well, your D3 is a little bit high," the doctor said. "Otherwise, everything looks fine."

My insurance eventually approved a visit with Dr. Z and I called to let her office know that I had hit a wall while racing. I followed up by sending an email as well and on January 11th, I went for a PET scan. The following day, we met with Dr. Z to go over the results.

"Your lower back is all lit up," she said after looking over the images from my scan. "The fractures in your spine are because the tumors have made the bone weak."

John and I sat there in shock. "Tumors?" I said. "What do you mean?"

"The cancer is back," my doctor replied. "And it's attacking your bones."

"But what about the car wreck?" I asked. "Couldn't that have caused the damage to my spine?"

"What car wreck?" Dr. Z replied. Apparently, in the pandemic chaos, my messages had not gotten through. I explained about dirt track racing and smashing into the wall with a loose harness. The look on my doctor's face told me she did not approve of this behavior.

"Breast cancer can travel through the bones," she told us. "I believe it's the tumors that have made your spine fragile."

"Then why were my other tests all normal?" I asked.

"Because they didn't understand the full scope of your diagnosis," Dr. Z replied.

With that, I was thrown back into the machine, more scans, tests and consultations, leaving me with more questions than answers. How could I go so quickly from remission and clear scans to a diagnosis of stage four cancer again? How could the damage in my spine come from cancerous lesions and not slamming a race car into a wall?

Even after all my research, I still could not understand the tumor thing. I was metastatic before, with lots of tumors attacking my body. This time around, the medical industry couldn't seem to land on a satisfactory explanation. Was it one big tumor? Several?

I'd had three consecutive scans that were completely clean, not that long before. Between that time and the crash did a rogue cancer cell go hog wild and attack my spine? Did the wreck break my back or did a tumor weaken my spine so much that any impact would have caused it to snap? And if the tumor was so aggressive, why had it seemed to stop growing now?

I started spending more time in meditation and prayer, working on visualizing God's healing and energy, on blood flowing through my body to the places where I needed it most. My previous regimen of adjunct therapy came back in full force, intense sessions in the infrared sauna, colonics, mushrooms and full spectrum CBD oil, which I feel helps my body absorb other medications and nutrients.

Dr. Z referred me to a group of surgeons who specialized in repairing damage to the spine. They reviewed my scans and saw that my back looked like a zigzag, with discs smashed flat rather than the donut shape they are supposed to be. "By the look of your X-Rays and MRIs, we thought they'd have to roll you in here in a wheelchair," the chief surgeon said.

The other surgeon was a young gun, a bit cockier in his approach. "You sure don't look like a stage four cancer patient to me," he said after studying my chart. "If you were a thirty-five-year-old female who fractured her spine picking up a sack of dog food, that would be a concern. But when a fifty-two-year-old woman hits a wall while racing cars and the only thing she breaks is her backbone...."

Considering that I also had a history of scoliosis and a previous spinal fracture from cheerleading when I was a teen, the young gun doctor didn't feel my damage was all that severe and that I was a good candidate for surgery. I liked this guy, but he was the junior partner in the practice and his supervising physician didn't want to go against my oncologist as far as treatment was concerned. He believed my bones weren't strong enough to endure all the plates and screws of a typical back surgery and that even if they did hold up, in the next few years, the bone could weaken and he would have to open me up and do the work all over again.

"It would be a vicious cycle," the surgeon said. "Treat the cancer first."

John and I continued to meet with physicians, hoping that someone could help us figure out what was going on so I could put together a plan of action. I returned to Vanderbilt's oncology department for a second opinion as well.

"Can't you do some kind of test to tell what it is?" I asked. "Is there a tumor we can start to target and shrink?"

The oncologist shook her head, no.

"So, what's lighting up my scans? Scar tissue? A broken bone?"

They didn't have an answer for that. Next, John and I met with a radiologist who explained that a bone splinter in my back could be the cause of my problems. "Imagine a stick in your swimming pool," the radiologist said. "Once it hits the skimmer, it's going to bounce around hitting things. It's possible that could be the root of all this pain."

Bear with me. I know this is a ton of doctors. That's part of the insanity and exhaustion of this kind of diagnosis. It seems like there's a doctor visit or result or test nearly every day and NONE of them appeared to be talking to each other. With every new visit, it felt like we had to plead our case all over again.

It's difficult to live the story, much less try to tell about it in a way that's not confusing.

John

I feel like the color commentator on play-by-play, bringing the reader up to speed. Alicia's back is broken, as evidenced by the X-rays and MRI. She also has a slipped and compressed disc, so much damage that I jokingly refer to her spine as "Jenga."

The oncologists are sending us to orthopedic surgeons and the surgeons are sending us back to the oncologists. Neither side can agree on a plan of treatment. The oncologist wants to do radiation, but not until the surgeon operates. The surgeon won't operate until the oncologist zaps the cancer.

Meanwhile, Alicia is in extreme pain, 24/7. She felt fine and had been doing great before the accident, so we didn't want to believe that the cancer had returned. Besides, the system had been wrong plenty of times before.

Alicia

This continued until finally, after a lot of back-and-forth chart notes, my team of doctors landed on the theory that I had compression fractures above and below a tumor. The oncologist and radiation doctor agreed: do back surgery first, then follow-up with chemo and radiation on the area.

The spinal surgeon disagreed. He didn't want to touch it. He believed that surgery might not even be necessary if we could get the tumor to shrink. I was stuck between opinions. No one seemed to be able to suggest a path of treatment. This time, there was no agreed upon "standard of care."

They did agree on this much: a piece of bone was lodged in my spinal cord, restricting blood flow and causing a tremendous amount of pain. My lower back was in bad shape and getting worse, but if we did surgery, there was a chance I could end up paralyzed. But if I didn't have it fixed, I was in danger of being paralyzed by any sort of fall or even a slight accident. Meanwhile, cancer had apparently seized the opportunity to return, only this time, clustered around my wounds.

One thing seemed certain: my house was on fire again. This time, the stakes were higher than ever before.

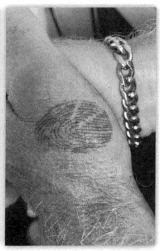

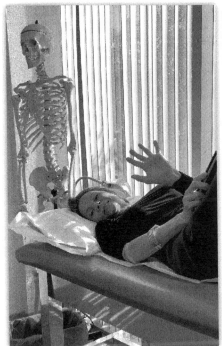

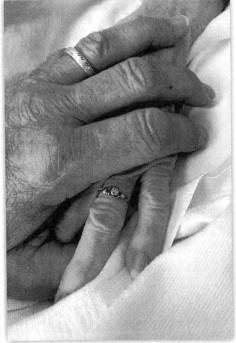

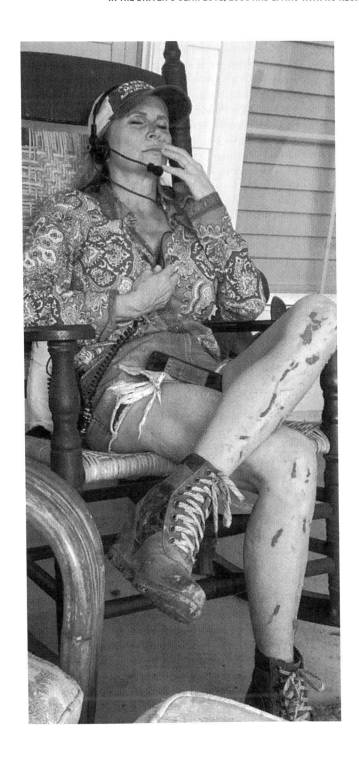

CHAPTER NINE
THE MACHINE

The pain became unbearable. Like, on a scale from one to ten, the constant stabbing and burning down my back and legs was a red hot, screaming thirteen. Opiates and muscle relaxers could get it down to an eight – but eight is still a miserable way to live and I was only able to manage an hour or two of sleep each night. John and I had just finished work on the *Poker Run* film and we were starting to put together plans for Bo's Extravaganza 2022, but my mind was too fogged by pills and fatigue to get much done.

I was frustrated by the process, encouraged by some new doctor or approach or test, then getting disappointed and confused, stuck because I couldn't find anyone who could give me a straight answer or the insight needed to change my situation. And I sure couldn't keep living that way.

John

Doctors can't fix everything. Modern medicine is a tool. It should never be the only tool in your box, nor was it meant to be. The best we can do as patients is to ask good questions and partner in the process of getting well and staying well. Never forget, you are your own best advocate.

Alicia

Due to our previous experiences, John and I remained skeptical while understanding that we couldn't let doubt keep us from moving forward. As a precautionary measure, I started back on the Ibrance and hormone therapy and jumped back into my studies so I could fine tune my adjunct attack, put it into high gear and try to make my cancer dog "sit and stay."

As I mentioned before, after experiencing a string of clean scans, I had eased off the keto diet and started having a glass of wine at night. On really crazy days, maybe two. Experts say the antioxidants in wine are good for you.

Sometimes with oncology, you get conflicting reports. One doctor said no liquor, period. Alcohol is an inflammatory that can weaken the immune system. Another oncologist didn't see a problem with wine at night, or even vodka since it's clean, low calorie and sugar-free.

So, what do you do? It's not even really about the alcohol, it's having that one little moment of peace and relaxation that you look forward to at the end of a difficult day. Cancer takes so much from you – and now it wants to take that away too? I don't want to make foolish choices. I don't want my doctors to say, "See, she doesn't listen. She brought this upon herself."

Aspirin was another thing I was warned about, due to the risk of increased bleeding. But some sources show that aspirin lowers the risk and side effects of cancer. When you are already under a mountain of stress, it's easy to be overwhelmed. There are so many small decisions in each day and when your health is at risk, you start second guessing everything. That's exhausting in itself.

I made the choice to cut back on alcohol and start the keto diet again. I continued to take aspirin in the form of BC Powders. When it felt like a big mad alligator was gnawing on my spine, BC Powders seemed to work faster. Besides, aspirin is made from bark and it's been around forever. That must be healthier than pain pills, right?

John was taking care of me, making connections, calling in favors and doing a lot of research on his own. He even went back on the diet with me, so he wouldn't be enjoying rice and gravy while I was doing my best with cauliflower chips and unsweet tea. We found this really good sugar-free bread and pickles at Trader Joe's and John would fix these amazing keto sandwiches. Maybe they were just amazing because he made them for me.

John
My God, I love this woman.

Alicia
One day, after a session in the infrared sauna, I tried to have a lymphatic massage but couldn't make it through. My body hurt all over, like a big, gnarly toothache and it felt like I was falling apart. We had been studying the benefits of magnet therapy, and the testimonies were positive enough for me to give it a try. The magnets supposedly increase blood flow and reduce inflammation. We even ordered a set of magnetic sheets.

Magnet therapy made my hip feel better, but the rest of my body felt like I'd been hit by a train. Further investigation showed that metal allergies can ramp up nerve pain. I'm sensitive to everything except for eighteen-karat or above gold and surgical steel. My nerves were already irritated and even the rivets on my jeans were causing them to flare up. Within thirty minutes of getting rid of the magnets, my symptoms went away, but the ordeal still messed with my mind.

When something goes wrong, your first impulse is to fear the worst. You can't even have a nosebleed without thinking, *that's it, I'm going to die,* worrying that the cancer is raging back, invading some other part of your body. I felt sure that God had fixed the problem before and I believe that once God fixes something, it's done. I'm not going to lie and tell you that my faith was always that strong. There were days when I got lost in the maze, believing the doctor's reports more than God's.

All I know is that I was doing great and then everything went crazy. In hindsight, I should have rushed to my oncologist immediately after the crash. If you are a cancer patient in remission and experience an accident or trauma, deal with it right away. Cancer is opportunistic. It sees trauma as an open door.

I still didn't have a satisfactory answer to my question – did a tumor weaken my bones and help cause a broken back – or did a car crash pave the way for cancer to return? Best I can understand, my PET scan would have still lit up from the fractures in my spine. Would the doctors have diagnosed it as cancer if I didn't have a history? Were the white spots on my scan metastasis or broken bones? In the world of oncology, it sometimes seems like everything suspicious or unidentified automatically gets branded as cancer until proven otherwise. Maybe that's a practical approach for oncologists, but it's scary as hell for patients.

Navigating the medical industry can be a such a grind. Long days of waiting in various depressing rooms, being poked and probed, people staring at your business in unflattering light. You feel so powerless.

It helped me to start looking at the relationship with my doctor like I would a hairdresser or banker. I need their input and expertise, but it's *my* hair. It's *my* money. And it is *my* health.

I want to build a relationship of trust with my medical team, but the bottom line is, nobody is going to advocate for my health and well-being more than me. As disappointing as it was to be thrown back into the fight, I knew that I had to fight cancer *my way*. I know I can be stubborn and difficult, but it's the only way I've ever been able to get things done. I had to take charge. I had to get back in the driver's seat – and stay there.

I began starting off appointments by going over a quick summary of my last visit with the doctor. Then, I would get them up to speed on everything that had happened since our last visit. Medical facilities can be intimidating. I've talked to many patients who feel overwhelmed and "just don't want to think about it." You cannot be passive in the face of disease. Find ways to take back your power and control. You must be informed and aware enough to take charge of the team that is fighting to get you well. Trust me, any good doctor wants their patient to be actively involved.

Have a list of questions ready for your next consult. Keep a file and a journal of progress. Charts are now online and the patient has full access. Read your chart. Take notes on anything you don't understand or want to discuss with your medical team. When we are anxious, depressed, or in pain, it's easy to let things slide, but you have to stay proactive. No one will take better care of you than *you*.

I eventually started recording meetings with the doctor on my phone so I could go over it later and always brought someone along to help be my eyes and ears. There's so much information in each visit that no one can remember it all. John and I review the visits right after. I want to know what he heard and make sure that I didn't miss anything important.

John

I love doctors. Some of my best friends are doctors. And yes, I've even played one on TV.

The medical industry is full of hardworking, caring people who truly want to help the sick. You just have to communicate and make sure that they are communicating with each other about your needs. If someone tells you that your house is on fire, you have a choice. You can run around screaming and crying while your house burns to the ground – or get to work putting out the fire.

At one point, we met with a doctor who specializes in integrative oncology. "What's the first thing a person who gets this diagnosis should do?" I asked.

"Treat it as if it's the flu," he replied. "Sure, it's bad. Yes, it can kill you. But you are not helpless against this. There are things that you can do."

Alicia and I determined to never refer to cancer as "the big C." We refused to give it that much power in our lives.

Alicia

For me, a big part of staying in the driver's seat is using the best of modern medicine combined with everything I can do concerning diet, supplements and changes in lifestyle. Even if your medical team is brilliant, accessible, and caring, it's important to remember that they are limited by strict legal and ethical guidelines. You can talk to your physicians about adjunct therapy but understand that is outside their scope of practice and expertise. They might even be against it. Adjunct treatment will likely be something you have to pursue on your own.

It's important to have people you can count on to guide you through the path. Find someone who's been where you are going and made it through the other side. If possible, it's helpful to have doctors who are outside of your treatment team to offer input as well.

Spiritual support is important too, a pastor, friends who will pray and lift you up. And once you make it through, God will call you to support, guide and help others. That's just as much an important part of adjunct therapy as any vitamin or supplement.

CHAPTER TEN
JUST KEEP GOING

The pieces of the puzzle were slowly coming together and evidence seemed to support that lesions had formed along my spine around the place of my injuries. Opinions continued to differ on the best course of treatment. This time, there was no "standard of care" and the barrage of tests continued.

One day, John and I had to wait two hours for an MRI. Each minute in the waiting room was torture, the pain in my back out of control. I don't sit still very well anyway, but I knew it was important for me to have that scan. As tempting as it was to get mad and leave, that would only cause more problems in the long run.

John

Alicia was biting her nails and I could tell she was in a lot of pain. I took her hand in mine and gave it a squeeze. "I guess this is another example of expect the best, prepare for the worst," I said.

"Right?" she replied. "Ain't that the truth."

My Smile had walked with me through the darkest time in my life and I wanted to be there for her in the same way.

Alicia

John's nickname for me has always been "my Smile," but in this season, he was mine, staying positive, holding on to the best and the good, always believing that I would overcome this. As hard as cancer can be on the patient, it's tough in a different kind of way for the spouse or parent or child or significant other. Back in the 80s, John had a hit song called "It's a Short Walk from Heaven to Hell" and I knew he was being dragged back into the fire too. But you know what they say about walking through hell . . . just keep walking.

In the medical business, lots of things can go wrong – and they will. There are always obstacles that you can never anticipate. Someone tells you of a great doctor, but after a lot of research and calls, you discover they don't take your insurance or aren't accepting new patients. You show up for a test and the machine is down. The scheduler made your appointment for the wrong day. Radiology didn't send over the right report. There's a new procedure that shows a lot of promise, but it's all out-of-pocket and the cost is way more than you could ever afford. Cancer is traumatic enough. Dealing with the medical industry is a trauma of another kind. Some days, I'm not sure which is worse.

It's easy to get flustered in such a place of vulnerability. I was already feeling sick, down and tempted to give up. But I couldn't quit. And that's frustrating too. After you get mad and sad and sick and tired of the entire crazy system, you know what you still have to do? Suck it up, buttercup. *Just keep walking.*

The next step in figuring out a treatment plan was a bone density test. At my age, it's normal to have a bit of bone loss. Dr. Z suggested that I was experiencing some atrophy in my legs due to the spinal injury. She tested my reflexes by thumping my knees with that little rubber doctor hammer. I might have been moving slow, but I knew I didn't have any atrophy.

"Okay," Dr. Z said, "I want you to kick me."

"Do what?"

She sat back, holding out her leg. "Kick me," she said again, almost like she was daring me.

How many chances do you get to kick your doctor? Especially when you are fed up with being passed around the medical system. I didn't kick hard as I could, but I laid it in there pretty good. Her eyes got wide as she bit her lip to keep from yelping.

"Was that okay?" I asked. "If you need me to, I can kick harder."

"That won't be necessary," Dr. Z replied.

The next day, I went to get my nails done, just to have a break and do something nice for myself. I shuffled into the nail salon, anxious and depressed, hanging on by a thread. I was leaning the chair back, trying to relax, when I accidentally hit the massager button and the Shiatsu rollers dug into my lower back, causing me to cry out in pain. The woman in the next chair looked over. "You okay, hon?"

"Yeah," I winced. "I just broke my back, so I'm having a hard time getting around."

"Girl, I can understand that," she said. "I got arthritis and compression on my spine."

As we talked, I realized our symptoms were the same. Arthritis grows in places of trauma too. That chance meeting felt like another confirmation. I'd found the right path before and beat this thing. Maybe that was the problem. In all the confusion, had I become distracted from my path?

As the pain wore on, my dependance on pain pills ramped up to dangerous levels. Hydrocodone led to oxycodone. The more you use opiates, the less they work. The only way I could make the pills kick in was to take them on an empty stomach. Then it was an empty stomach with a shot of alcohol.

I tried dry needling, visits with a chiropractor and a series of "shotgun blast" spinal injections or epidurals. The relief was short-lasting, at best. It was a full-time job to try and fight the pain.

John

Was I scared? Hell, yes, I was. But if I ever let it show, Alicia was quick to tell me to "suck it up!" In the heat of battle, she was the one encouraging me. I wasn't about to let the woman I loved more than myself know that I was afraid I might lose her. No way, not me, not John Wayne Schneider.

But between you and me? I have never been so scared in my life.

Alicia

If that weren't enough, I started having issues with my kidneys, so I made an appointment to see a urologist. Another new doctor added to the list. He went in with a scope and did a contrast. "Your left kidney is at about twenty percent," the doctor said.

The blood drained from my face before I had the courage to ask. "Do you think it could it be cancer?"

"Let's not jump the gun," he said, game face on. "It might be scar tissue since you've had a history of kidney issues before. Since you don't have lymph nodes in that area, I find it hard to believe the cancer could move there."

Dr. Z ordered yet another PET scan to check for any issues. The tumors weren't growing or spreading, but they weren't shrinking either. I was on autopilot, eyes vacant, lost. Maven Entertainment has many divisions – music, films, appearances, memorabilia, a studio for hire. I supervise about eight crews and hit the ground running every day, booking agent, manager, and all-around chief firefighter.

Not anymore. I could barely hold meetings, stooped over in pain, staring up at whoever I was talking with at the time. We put everything on hold except the bare minimum of events until I could get myself to a better place. An indie business lives off the next gig. Suddenly, we had a lot of money going out, not much coming in, and a lot of pressure to catch up and reschedule things now that Covid was finally coming to an end. Work ethic is important to me. I had always been able to push through before, but it was getting harder to keep my nose to the grindstone.

Keto wasn't a problem since I could only hold down a few bites a day. Then oxycodone led to fentanyl. The next thing I knew, I weighed ninety-six pounds. Nearly twenty pounds under my "danger" weight of one-fourteen.

One of my doctors told John that it might be wise to hide my guns. He was right. I'd hit rock bottom and my mind had turned to escape, calling out to God, *please, just get me out of this.* Those who judge have never been there. Pain will make you consider very desperate things.

Even in the worst of it, I kept believing God had a better way, kept believing that there was someone out there who could help me. John was making calls and reaching out to every contact he had for some spark of hope. Being married to the co-founder of the Children's Miracle Network is a good asset in a medical disaster. Maybe you don't have that kind of connection, but most of us have some link or access and in a crisis, you must use every advantage you have to fight.

Through a mutual connection, an orthopedist that specialized in sports medicine got in touch with us. "Listen, I'm one of the top surgeons in Louisiana," he began. "But your problem is beyond our local capabilities."

He referred me to his mentor, a specialist in spinal tumors at MD Anderson back in Houston. I'd been wanting to go back to MD Anderson anyway, because they have the best technology and are one of the few oncology facilities that believe in adjunct therapy. I had prayed for God to show us the next step and that was confirmation enough for me.

The doctors back home had been pushing for me to start radiation. Oncologists tend to want to rush you into a frenzy of treatment. We all want to be good patients, but I don't believe that's always the right thing to do. If I had jumped into every recommendation, I would have already lost my breasts and been through more than one harsh round of chemo and radiation. I believe I might have even lost my life.

Radiation was something I was willing to wait and push back on. It can be palliative or curative and at that point, I was in enough pain to be a little more open to it than I had been before. Still, I was really hoping to avoid going down that road.

We met with the spine specialist in Houston. Finally, we had someone who knew spines and tumors both. He looked over my scans, consulted with an oncologist at MD Anderson and gave me his opinion straight. Address the damage to my back first but wait on surgery for the time being and try a few more options to deal with the excruciating pain.

As John stood and shook his hand, the surgeon pulled him in close. "Whatever you do," he whispered, "don't radiate."

John nodded. The doctor was giving us a much-needed nugget of truth. But I already had a long list of things I shouldn't or couldn't do and I still wasn't any closer to finding a path and a way to move on.

CHAPTER ELEVEN
GET UP

At our 2022 Bo's Extravaganza, John was out doing "A Ride with Bo." It's a fun event. A fan gets to ride shotgun with "Bo Duke," in the General Lee, tearing down a backroad, straightenin' the curves and flattenin' the hills. John answers questions and tells stories about the car and his life. I think he might even pull a few 180s, as long as the law isn't around.

As John and the fan were driving, talk turned to health struggles and chronic pain. The fan told John about a surgeon in Florida who didn't believe in screws or fusions to fix a person's back, using lasers instead of a knife. John raced back into the house all excited, but I wasn't in the mindset to deal with yet another experimental treatment option or some new doctor with a new idea.

I was doing my best to run the Extravaganza from bed, trying to keep our crew and events on schedule, trying to manage my anxiety and pain. Thousands of fans were crowded onto the grounds of our studio, John was jumping a Dodge Hellcat a hundred-and-fifty feet into a pile of boxes and even from a lying position, it was taking everything I had to keep the wheels from falling off.

Finally, John, in all his tenacity and optimism, gets this Florida doctor on the phone. Then, he sticks his phone in my face and says, "Talk."

I took John's phone with a roll of my eyes. "Hi, this is Alicia," I said.

"Hello, Alicia, this is Dr. B. in Florida. Are you familiar with laparoscopic lasers?"

"Back in Los Angeles, they used lasers to clean my teeth," I replied.

"That's one of the things they're used for, yes," he said. "About thirty years ago, I developed a technique where I can use lasers to do the same thing to your spine."

He had my attention then. We spoke about my condition for about a half-hour before I had to pull it together, put on my best face and be Mrs. Bo Duke with John for the Extravaganza's VIP meet-and-greet. Once we'd finished taking pictures, I told John, "I think this doctor can help me. We need to meet him face-to-face."

"Alright, then," John said with a nod. "We'll leave for Florida tomorrow."

That's my husband. Work all night and day, jump a Hellcat for the fans, catch a couple hours sleep and get back on the road to help me find some help.

The next day, we were east bound on I-10, headed down to Tampa Bay. The Bellamy Brothers had just headlined Bo's Extravaganza, so we parked our camper at their family farm in nearby Darby the night before my appointment. The Bellamys are old hippies, living off the land, very much into natural medicine.

The next morning, David Bellamy whipped up some concoction of herbs in hot tea while his wife, Susan, applied a medicinal rub to my legs and back. I take CBD, but I'm a lightweight. Especially when I can't eat much and weigh under a hundred pounds.

By the time John and I pulled up to the doctor's office, I was ten miles high and flying, feeling more than a little bit paranoid and whacked out. The clinic was super-nice, lots of glass and mirrors and high-end furniture. "John, John, this place is, like, Beverly Hills," I said pulling on his sleeve and talking too fast. "We don't need to be here spending money we don't have."

Insurance doesn't cover experimental procedures, so treatment would all be out of pocket and the Bellamy's home-brewed remedies already had me on edge. I wasn't being much of a good patient, more like a snarky teen, refusing to give out my social security number or date of birth, refusing X-rays, fidgeting and unable to keep still. THC is supposed to be great for cancer patients but it makes me crazy. Plus, I was already skeptical after all the doctors and tests and blood draws and opinions I had been through.

John tried to calm me down enough to get in the machine and take an MRI. He flipped on his phone camera and recorded me in the waiting room. "Say hello, Alicia," he said.

I shot him the side-eye. "Hello." I giggled nervously, leg bouncing, perched on the edge of my seat.

"I need you to be still for twenty minutes so they can do your MRI," John said calmly. "Can you do that?"

"I don't know," I replied. "Depends on the pain."

"Well, I need you to try," he said.

"Okay," I said. "But you know what's the most important thing?"

"What's that?"

"Have fun," I said. "Whatever we do, we have to find a way to make it fun."

John laughed. "Say goodnight, Gracie."

I laughed back. That's our little in-joke. We're a like a modern-day George and Gracie, Desi and Lucy, Cary Grant and Mae West. I felt a little calmer as I put on the gown. Crazy as it sounds, somehow, we were making it fun.

I made it through the MRI and Dr. B. and his team came in for the initial consultation. He talked about studying acupuncture techniques in Asia and said he could go in without having to make big incisions or any use any metal or concrete. While the other doctors I met with focused on my spine, B.'s team felt the source of pain was my SI joint, which sits just below your lower back and above your tailbone.

"Let's try something," B. said. "Lay flat on your stomach."

I was still dubious but with John's help, I got up on the exam table and laid down. With a long needle, B. injected the area around my SI joint with lidocaine. Even with my high tolerance for pain, it hurt like hell. But then, I felt instant relief.

"Okay, get up," he said.

"Are you kidding?" I asked. "My back is broken. I can't get off this table without help."

He said it again, firmer. "Get up."

I scooched to the edge of the table and pushed with my arms, slowly swinging my legs to the side and bracing for the lightning bolts of pain to shoot through me. No pain. I stood. Still didn't hurt. I could move, better than I had in ages.

"Do you trust me now?" the doctor asked.

My paranoia vanished with the pain. "Yes sir," I replied.

"Okay, we'll do the first procedure tomorrow," he said, pointing to the spot where he'd just stuck the needle in. "And that's where we'll begin."

CHAPTER TWELVE
BLAZING TRAILS

By the next day, I felt much more clear-headed and hopeful. Before the surgery, Dr. B. explained that his infrared laser could work on about two inches of bone at a time and that I would stay awake throughout the procedure. Large monitors were mounted around the surgery center and I watched as Dr. B. made a tiny incision and slid the laser and camera through my skin and down to my SI joint where he began to locate the metastasis and burn them to death.

Following the surgery, I was still hurting, but significantly less than before. "Okay," Dr. B. said. "Try to do something that you could not do before."

"Really?"

B. nodded. Slowly, I lifted my right leg. Then my left.

"I can pick up my legs," I told him, lifting the right one again, higher this time. "I haven't been able to do that in months."

But each time, a new pain emerged. The tumors were vanishing, but the damage to the bones and ligaments remained. The next day, I had surgery again, continuing to focus on the lesions in my SI joint down to the tailbone, the areas causing me the most pain.

"All right," Dr. B. said. "Do something you couldn't do before."

I stood and bounced from one foot to the other, tapping heel and toe. "You're tap dancing?" he said.

"You know how long it's been since I could dance?" I asked.

In the days ahead, we continued to work and after each surgery, he would have me do something new. Following the next procedure, I was able to get into pike position, hands on the floor, legs straight, hips high in the air. I used to love yoga, but it had been a very long time since I could even do the simplest stretch.

From there, I took a new set of MRIs to share with my oncologists. They looked them over carefully, curious, but ultimately dismissive of the results. I think it was too far outside their standard of practice and comfort zone.

I'd faced many crossroads in treatment and the decision was never an easy one to make. Who do I trust? Which path do I take? Lasering cancerous metastasis is an experimental procedure, but somebody has to go first and I'd already lived beyond the five-year marker for my diagnosis. I don't mind being the crash test dummy. I like blazing trails. If it could help me and possibly help others, then I believe that's what God has called me to do.

John

This process was amazing to watch. Dr. B. was clear in stating that he didn't know if any of this would work on Alicia's cancer, but that felt certain he could help her with the pain.

"You deal with the pain and we'll deal with the cancer," I told him. "That little lady in there is not only ten feet tall, but she's tougher than a Waffle House steak."

Later, Alicia said, "If this doesn't work for me, that doesn't mean we didn't learn anything. Take it and keep going. Eventually, it'll work for someone."

Alicia

I'm not going to act like the decision was simple, but I knew how I felt before and how I felt after – and that was enough for me. B.'s procedure had taken my pain level from sky high to manageable with a few simple surgeries that required no heavy anesthesia or stitches and screws and rods and a long recovery time. And, in doing so, he had given me hope, at least for a better quality of life while I was fighting.

"I'm in," I told him. "Don't stop now. Let's keep going."

From there, we were off, scanning and mapping the best course of attack. For my next surgery, the team lasered tumors off my hip bones. After all the destruction that cancer had caused, it was pretty satisfying to watch it get destroyed instead and soon enough, my pain level had dropped enough to where I could pull away from the opiates.

In September, John and I flew from Nashville to Tampa Bay for what should have been my final surgery to remove lesions from my bones. Once again, I watched the surgeon make a half-inch incision at the bottom of my back and use his laser to burn the tumors from the L5-S1 area of my spine.

"The operation was successful," B. said after he closed me back up. "But during the procedure, I nicked the outer portion of your spinal cord. So, to be safe, I want you to stay very still for the next few days."

"Aw, no water skiing?" I joked.

"No skiing," he laughed. "No dancing. No stairs. Lay still. Rest."

From there, they wheeled me down the hall for a follow-up MRI to check my progress.

The technician said that although the scan looked good, we wouldn't really know until the radiologist could compare my pre-surgery images side by side with the new ones. I nodded back, thankful. But the pain monster was already beginning to wake up and as always, he was seriously pissed.

Dr. B. insisted that I be transported home by ambulance. The staff moved me from the exam table to one of those flat spinal boards like you see paramedics use at car wrecks. They lifted me up and plopped me down on the board – just a few inches – and I screamed like the shower scene in *Psycho*. I think they heard me all the way from Tampa to Space Mountain. Pain shot down my legs, radiating into my toes and back up to the top of my head. It was worse than the car crash that had broken my back in the first place!

The nurses ran to get Dr. B.. At first, he wanted to open me back up to check the packing he put around my spine after the surgery. "No, no, *please* don't do that," I begged. "I wasn't hurting after I got off the surgery table, so maybe it'll settle back down."

B. reluctantly agreed to watch and wait. I took one low-dose hydrocodone, just enough to take the edge off. Finally, the pain dropped to an acceptable level and I was able to make the trip home and rest.

My back was still as mess from a lifetime of scoliosis and car crashes, but I figured I could manage that with yoga, Pilates, and lots of laughter and prayer. If we could just get rid of the tumors again, I could take the next step.

John had a booking that we couldn't reschedule, so he headed out while I stayed at the house and tried not to overthink things. After three days of bed rest, the spinal team remove packing from the surgery site. The next day, I flew back to Louisiana to wait for the results. The following Friday, I received the call.

"Your tests are back," the doctor said.

"Is it good news?" I asked.

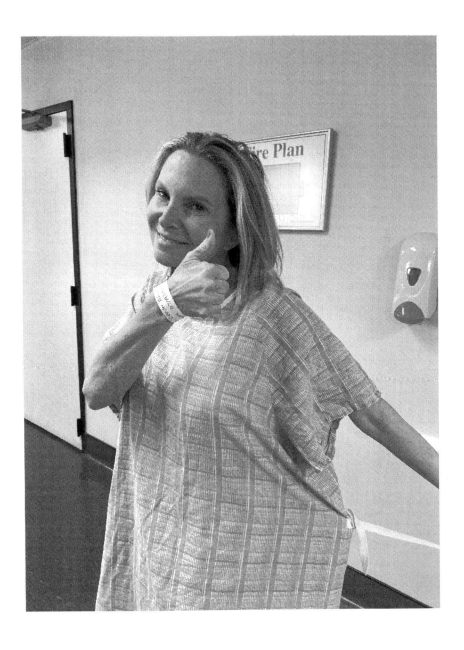

CHAPTER THIRTEEN
STAY IN THE FIGHT

After sixteen surgeries in seven months, the side-by-side MRI comparison showed a significant reduction in bone abnormality. There were a lot of other medical terminology and measurements, but all in all the news was good.

Dr. B. was pleased and John was elated. I was trying to balance hope and reality, believing for the best while still fighting fear and my dubious nature. Have faith, believe in miracles, but do so while living in truth rather than denial. A healthy dose of caution and skepticism helps you to stay in control.

Even though my scans showed progress, there were still a few "dirty" spots on the MRI around my sit bone and SI joint. I was still having pain in those places too.

"Your vertebrae look good," Dr. B. said. "If you're okay with it, I believe I can go back in, do a little touch-up and work on pain management."

"Sure," I told him. "Have I really got much to lose?"

I stayed awake, just taking in oxygen and a small hit of anesthesia here and there to stay calm. Once the surgery was done, they took me into the recovery room. "Okay, try a few squats," B. said.

I was able to do them, but still had some stiffness and pain. The surgery suite was already shut down, but B. opened it up to go back in again. We didn't have time to set up X-rays for laser guidance or the anesthesiologist to prep. "Just go," I told the team. "I can handle it. We need to get this done."

I was able to breathe deep, pray and guide him to the sources of pain. I could hear the *zap zap zap* of the laser and at one point, someone in the room gasped. I guess it's pretty rare to have surgery without anesthesia? After everything I'd been through in the last year, I would have bit a .38 bullet while the surgeon went in with a hacksaw if it would have helped with the pain.

"You're so strong," one of the team told me once we were done. "You are a superhero."

"No, I'm not super anything," I replied. "There's a reason I'm here. God is getting me through this so I can help others get through too."

John

Alicia's being humble. I was there, watching. She's Superwoman.

Alicia

I crashed hard that night, sleeping sound for the first time in ages. To celebrate, John ordered me a pepperoni pizza with thick, gooey crust. My weight had crept back up over a hundred. I was feeling good and could finally see an end to the intense fighting.

I still did the keto diet but started to cycle on and off. There's a time and season for everything. Sometimes your body needs time to breathe. And now and then, it needs a good dose of carbs, pepperoni and cheese.

The lymph nodes and white blood cell count looked good when my labs came back. My OB/GYN and radiology oncologist felt the results were impressive and encouraged me to carry on. John packed up our camper to make the drive from Florida to California for the birth of our first grandbaby. Nobody on my medical team thought it was a good idea to take such a long trip that soon after surgery, but I was determined not to miss it.

John

Did I mention that Alicia can be stubborn? And maybe a little impetuous?

Alicia

While John drove cross-country, I laid on the couch behind him and cried for thirty hours. Tenacity is a gift and curse. My team was right. It was too soon after surgery. All my life, I've pushed. There's still a big part of me that thinks, *I don't have time to be sick. I've got too many things to do. Get it fixed and move on!*

I had always been good at mind over matter before, shutting out the noise to do what needs to be done. Pain demands attention. It got so loud that I could not rise above or drown it out.

I'd been working on a better relationship with John's daughter, Karis, and wanted to be there so badly for her and to be a good "GiGi" for baby Sierra Lynn. I knew it probably wouldn't be long before my daughter was expecting too. Pain also gives you perspective. Life's too short and family is too important. We consider them both our daughters.

Time moves so quickly. Seems like just the other day I was a young mother, trying to do my best, trying to make it in the movie business and be a mama and daddy for my daughter too. Back then, I pushed like crazy.

A deep south girl in Hollywood leaning on Marlboro Reds, Diet Coke and Jesus. Hey, don't judge. Most of y'all have been there too, doing whatever it takes to get through the day. I'd bounce that baby girl on my hip and she would look into my eyes with that all-knowing, read-your-soul innocence and I knew in my heart, *I gotta quit smoking these frickin' cigarettes.*

But how? I never thought I could live without smoking. Remember that fourteen-year-old cheerleader leading police on a high-speed chase in her boyfriend's Mercedes? You just know she's pulling on a Marlboro, right? It was love at first puff. But every time I looked at Baby Jess, it tore me apart. I knew I had to give it up.

A friend in the business referred me to a hypnotherapist in Santa Monica named Kerry Gaynor that specialized in helping people quit cigarettes. Hypnosis might sound like voodoo to some, but I believe it's just basic spiritual principles. The Bible tells us to take every thought captive, that we are what we think and to change our lives, first, we must change our minds.

Kerry simply taught me how to plant the seeds to aim my focus and my thoughts in a better direction. I wasn't strong enough to do it for myself, but I could quit smoking for Jessica. In three sessions, I put down cigarettes and never picked them up again.

This time, it wasn't cigarettes that I needed help to overcome. I was struggling with a form of panic attacks. I called it a "pain attack," the fear of oncoming pain and losing control. You get beat down enough and you learn to fear the next punch to the face. Then you start fearing the fear. I knew I had some things to unlearn and I knew I wasn't strong enough to do it myself.

Kerry stays booked out for months at a time and it had been over twenty years since I'd been to his office. I didn't have the strength or presence of mind for my usual persistence – but John did. He reached out to at least give it a try. Kerry just happened to have a rare cancellation and said he could see me right away.

Kerry's office looked the same as it had in the nineties and he was still the same calm, friendly but professional person he was back then. I told him my story, everything that I had been through, beating cancer back in 2019 and how much I was still beating myself up for getting in that race car crash.

I need to stop and tell you how important it is to have somebody just listen, someone who will let you tell your story with all the tears and doubt and fears, without having it all together or figured out. There are plenty of people who will throw Bible verses at you or cliches about how to handle hard times. Or plenty who want to give you tips or tell you about their cousin or neighbor or ex-brother-in-law who beat lung cancer by drinking lemon juice and kerosene. Another important part of adjunct therapy is finding people who know how to listen and make you feel heard.

Anyway, back to Kerry Gaynor. After I told my story, he gave me some key insights and affirmations, planting good seeds and giving me skills to move forward. More than twenty years later, he helped me find center again.

Once the session was over, I felt at peace for the first time in many days. That was an affirmation too: follow peace. Easier said than done. It really does take a team. God plants people in your life, but it's up to us to respond.

"I'm putting together a lifeboat to get through this storm," I told Kerry. "Will you be one of my people in it?"

"A lifeboat," Kerry said with a nod of approval. "Of course."

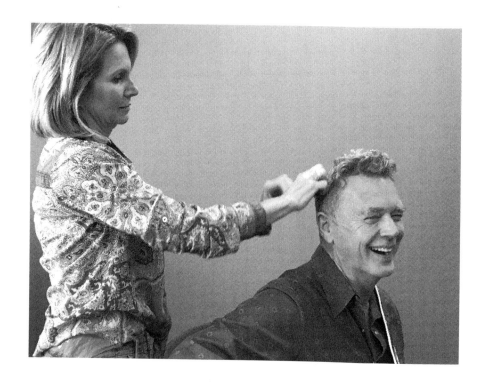

CHAPTER FOURTEEN
THE LIFEBOAT

It was four-thirty sundown in South Louisiana and I was sitting with my friend, Lannie, by the outdoor fireplace, drinking coffee, trying to wake up and work the stiffness out of my legs and back. We were catching up, but my phone kept going off, dates to book, plans coming together for movies and music and shows.

"I just bought a food truck," I told Lannie, showing her the pic as I hung up.

"Why y'all need a food truck?"

"For the drive-in theatre we're opening in the field by the barn."

"How do you run five businesses while brainstorming four more and still find the strength to fight stage four cancer?" Lannie said with a shake of her head. "Don't you ever stop to smell the roses?"

I smiled and sat back. "These *are* my roses," I said.

Lannie and I have known each other since we were kids. She became a nurse and then went on to become a nurse practitioner. We talk a lot about medical issues and life in general.

"I guess I've always known how to pull a team together to get things done," I explained. "I've got different people in different categories and it's mostly figuring out who gets a seat in my lifeboat."

Lannie took a long sip and nodded like she was thinking over what I'd said. "Think you can draw that for me?" she asked.

I'd never put it on paper before. It's in my head. Family, friends. Professional connections. Friends who cross over into the professional. I had a film lifeboat and a music lifeboat, another for fighting cancer. As I began to map out how they all fit together, I realized the importance of boundaries and support. There's something powerful about getting a concept out of your head and seeing it on paper.

"See, you're in two boats," I told Lannie, turning the sheet of paper so she could see the names and labels. "You're my trusted friend and I trust your opinion with the medical stuff. I know I can always depend on you to be on my side."

After our visit, I started taking a closer look at my lifeboat. When you are holding on for dear life, you need a crew you can count on in a storm, people who are low maintenance, dependable, ones you can trust to shoot straight and not just tell you what you want to hear.

There are others who, for whatever reason, fall to the side. They can't keep a secret or stir up too much drama or simply never show up on time. I'm not saying you don't love them. Or that you leave them to drown. But in a crisis, you cannot afford to be weighed down.

Sometimes the people in your life may need to be repositioned. Support is too important to leave to chance or waste time playing nice. You can be on the shore, but you cannot have a seat in my boat. Round two of this fight has taught me the importance of a good team of people who are rowing in the same direction.

John

Beware of doctors who don't want to hear what other doctors have to say. Beware of anyone – no matter how good their intentions might be – who pulls you away from your focus, goals and ability to move forward. Believe me, you cannot afford to be distracted.

Alicia

Round two had knocked me down, but I was ready to move on. I felt certain that the cancer in my bones was gone, but my hips and lower back were still giving me a lot of discomfort. One night, I was tossing and turning in bed, unable to rest. "Tell me what it feels like," John said, flicking on his phone camera. "Help me understand."

"Like . . . burning needles," I groaned. "Like fire shooting down into my legs and feet."

John kept filming, asking me questions, pushing me to be as specific as I could be. Then he sent the video to Dr. B.

"Okay, those issues are mechanical," B. replied. "I think I can help with that."

The next day, we headed back to Florida so the team could go in again, this time to work on the functional issues in my hips and lower back. I'm glad their recovery room is really nice because there's no telling how many hours I spent in there. Dr. B. came in after the procedure to check on how

I was feeling.

"Okay," he said. "Can you do something you couldn't do before?"

I grinned back. We'd been through the routine many times before. After moving around and stretching a bit, I nodded. "Yeah," I replied. "For the first time in ages, I can say that my legs and back don't hurt."

John

Let me rewind a bit so I can add something. One day, after seeing multiple metastasis on Alicia's MRI, I asked Dr. B. if he were familiar with poison ivy.

"Not really," he said.

"The way to kill all the poison ivy on one root is to wilt it with a little heat," I told him. "Because if you blast the leaves with flame, the poison ivy panics and go into self-preservation mode. Fight or flight. Later, it'll come right back, only this time, much stronger."

"Okay...," Dr. B. replied.

"What if the tumor is the root and the metastasis are poison ivy leaves?" I said. (I did play a doctor on TV once, you know.)

B. thought for a minute before turning to his assistant surgeon. "Can we adjust the temperature on the laser?"

"Sure," the surgeon said. "From zero to six thousand degrees."

"Let's try two hundred. I know right where we'll test John's poison ivy theory."

Alicia had a metastasis on her C2 and another on her C4. Theoretically, both metastases are on the same "root" system. While she and I watched the screens, Dr. B. made the metastasis on C2 "uncomfortable" with much less heat than he usually used.

On the subsequent MRI, the metastasis on C2 was clear . . . but so was the one on C4! The spot he didn't laser was gone too. I have to believe this will lead to a breakthrough in cancer treatment someday.

Alicia

My bones were clear, but I wasn't out of the woods yet. Remember the kidney thing? With the volume of my back and hip pain turned down, I could hear my kidneys screaming. Turns out that I had a mass of scar tissue blocking my urethra. Under the knife again. A friend joked that I must be going for the record of most surgeries in a year.

More doctors. More post-op pain to maneuver. More of the cancer panic and scans that goes with every health scare.

I was recovering from surgery when the news came in that Dr. Z was closing her local practice. Lady of Lakes, Vanderbilt, MD Anderson – I lost all three of my original oncologists. We didn't even mention the others in this book because there are already so many doctors at different locations, so many opinions and miles spent driving down dead-end roads that I didn't want to make the story even more confusing than it already is.

I started thinking about my journey so far. We were blessed to be able to see multiple oncologists at different top-notch facilities. Most people just have that one doctor they depend upon. Since my diagnosis, I'd spoken with a lot of people battling cancer who lost their primary doctor. You're in the middle of a war and next thing you know, the captain of your platoon retires and rides off into the sunset.

As a patient, how would I feel if that one person in the driver's seat was leaving? I thought about all the faces I saw in waiting rooms, people who were depending on that one medical professional to save their lives. I wondered how hopeless and scared many of them must feel.

You spend years building a trusting relationship and suddenly, that person is gone. I understand that jobs change and families move. All I'm saying is thank God I stayed informed and in charge of my treatment. If your lifeboat is strong, you can withstand the loss of one member of your crew.

CHAPTER FIFTEEN
MOVING ON

A friend told me about Sister Dulce Maria, a nun in Baton Rouge with a ministry of prayer and healing. I had known of her for a couple of years and wanted to visit, but her schedule is so tight that's it's nearly impossible to get in. Still, I reached out, praying that something might open up soon. When she called to say I should come over, I took that as an appointment from God and made the drive to Cypress Springs Prayer Center in Baton Rouge.

Sister Dulce is a tiny woman with glasses and a big smile in a habit so clean and white that it looks like she's glowing. Actually, she does glow, with so much joy and peace that I didn't even notice her wheelchair. At first, I thought, *if she's a healer, why is she in a wheelchair?* After you meet her, you don't think that anymore. It's all God and God is all good and Sister Dulce is quick to mention how he uses imperfect things to bring glory to his name.

I sat beside her, waiting, not mentioning anything about my condition. She held my hands and told me about the problems in my back and spine, the things that I had been through, mentioning specific details, some that even the X-rays and MRI scans could not see.

"You are very strong," Sister Dulce said. "Maybe the strongest person I have ever met. God is using you through this trial and because you've been faithful, he will continue to strengthen you to do the work he has called you to do."

I didn't feel strong. I felt tired. But if I am strong, it's because I do feel called, and if you're called, you don't stop and you never give up. Strength is built through struggle and resistance. The mission is bigger than you.

Then Sister Dulce prayed, calling God "Papa," asking for healing and peace and clarity, all the things I so badly need. She said, "Amen," and then grasped my fingers and looked deeply into my eyes. "Watch out for people who don't believe in what you are doing," she said. "Let nothing or no one hold you back. You have a great work to do for God."

On the drive home, I played her words over again in my head. I grew up Catholic. I've been to a lot of different churches since then, Southern

Baptist, Pentecostal, Nondenominational, Church of Christ. Every church has problems because every church is full of messy people. Those things we argue about are so petty. Especially when you're facing a life-threatening illness. We all belong to God.

Sister Dulce Maria confirmed the importance of keeping my lifeboat on course. Seems like everything I've been through in the last four years has re-inforced that point. Be kind, be open to learn and change – but you cannot afford to be passive when your house is on fire.

Life is just a series of fires, isn't it? I've always been good at putting out fires, stepping in to solve problems, helping someone figure out a solution and a plan. It's different when the house in flames is your own. I've learned some hard lessons about holding on and letting go, when to push and when to pull back. God is in control, but he left us in charge. Faith comes with responsibility.

I try my best to take it day by day, celebrating the small moments and victories, releasing uncertainties to God. Seems there's always a new challenge on the horizon, a consultation or exam or test to make sure my cancer cells haven't gone into rebellion again.

When I was first diagnosed in 2019, the doctors rushed me into a crisis plan to try and get a handle on things. MD Anderson noted on my last scan that the progression was "mild." I'm hoping that's a positive sign. Cautious optimism seems to be the best path forward.

That might have been part of problem before. Too much optimism, not enough caution.

After I beat cancer the first time, I pulled back on some of my treatments. The maintenance takes over your life and you just want to move on to brighter things. Adjunct therapy can be just as confusing as mainstream medicine. There are so many theories and cure-alls and various roads to travel. No cancer is alike and every person is different. It takes a lot of trial and error to figure out what your body responds to, what's worth spending your money and efforts on.

Back in 2019, I put a lot of prayer and study into choosing my protocols. I took it as confirmation from God when my girlfriend showed up the morning of on my wedding day to tell me, "You are on the right path." I still draw on those words for strength and confirmation, but sometimes I wonder, *did I get off the path somehow? Why did everything go wrong?*

I've also figured out that it's okay to get frustrated with God sometimes. God can handle my anger. He knows what it's like to be human. As long as I don't sit in my anger and let it paralyze me or make me bitter. Once I get beyond the frustration and anger, I realize I still need God's help and grace to get me through. I am not nearly strong enough on my own.

My diagnosis is a life-long fight. I've got to stay on my toes, stay centered and stay close to God. In racing, it's important to set your sights on the road ahead. Whether I've got a thousand miles to go or just a few, I know what waits for me on the other side. Better still, I know *who* waits for me.

Until then, I'm excited to dream and live life again. My goal and guide for the future is peace and calm. Our daughter is getting married soon. I want to be an asset and not a liability, vibrant, capable, strong. I want to be there for Jess, not for her to have to worry about me. I want to be there for our grandkids. My grandmother is ninety-eight and still going strong. I have every expectation to live that long.

John

I'll be a hundred and seven by then, but I plan on sticking around and keeping you honest. Besides, we've got so many plans and things to do, it'll take us at least that long. We'll still be the team to beat, baby.

Alicia

John has been so supportive through this. God knows, we'd already been through so much hell. Instead of running away at the news of a stage four diagnosis, he ran towards the fire – by buying a ring, getting down on one knee and asking me to be his wife. Since that time, he's driven me thousands of miles, sat through countless doctor's appointments, and kept me going when I didn't have the strength to keep going on my own.

It's been a wild ride. A little too wild at times. So, our number one objective for the future is to enjoy life more. In eight years together, we've only taken a few vacations. I want to take real vacations, not just traveling for doctor visits and tour dates. John and I want to be less of a production company and more of a husband and wife who have a lot of fun together.

Part of our fun is doing projects. There are plenty of those to keep us busy. Soon, we'll start filming *Double or Nothing*, the final film in the *Stand on It!* trilogy. We're both passionate about a project called *The Corridor*, which is about human trafficking and drug smuggling from Mexico to Miami. That's our neck of the woods and we've heard a lot of heart-breaking stories.

And we still plan to make our *Winner Takes All* movie, although at this point, it's almost become a documentary. Thank God John shot plenty of footage of me on the track. I don't think I'll be getting back in that race car again. There is a little red Fiero waiting on our studio lot though. Sure would be fun to be a teenager again, sunroof open, wind in my hair with all of life in front of me and not a care in the world....

John and I were headed back from Florida the other day, talking about movies, when suddenly I realized something. In most of John's films, he plays a widower, trying to get his life back on track after the loss of his spouse.

"What's that about?" I asked.

"It makes for a good story," he explained.

"Let's make a new story," I told him. "One with a strong female lead. One who lives and loves life and leaves an impact."

John flashed that famous smile as he steered us back onto the open road. "Sounds good to me," he said.

ROUND III: REDEFINING VICTORY

"He will wipe every tear from their eyes.
There will be no more death or crying or pain, f
or the old order of things has passed away.
He who was seated on the throne said,
"I am making everything new!"
- Revelation 21: 1-7

Alicia Ann Allain Schneider passed away at her home surrounded by family as she took her last breath on Tuesday, February 21, 2023. She was a native of Brusly and resident of Holden.

Alicia is survived by her husband, John R. Schneider, who he called "My Smile;" her daughter, Jessica Ann Dollard (Daniel Turner) who she was very proud of, and soon-to-be-born grandson Michael Shepherd Turner; parents, Michael and Linda Marino Allain; brother, Brandy Michael Allain; grandmother, Doris Crutti Marino Alvarado; stepdaughter, Karis Schneider (Justin); granddaughter, Sierra Schneider.

From Brusly to Hollywood and back, Alicia was a force that inspired others, kind and generous to all, a true servant who always put herself last. She was very protective of her parents, family and close friends, a mama bear that protected all her cubs. She was a fighter until the end.

To respect the family's privacy, a private service will be held. In lieu of flowers, please say prayers for her surviving family. Hug your loved ones, hold them tight and tell them how much you love and appreciate them. Life is far too short and precious for anything else.

Jamie Blaine

The co-writer's place is behind the scenes, so feels like I should give a little background before I speak. I'm a small-town southern boy who got a scholarship to study behavioral psych, moved to Nashville and became a writer. I like behind the scenes, digging into the story to tell a deeper truth.

Dukes of Hazzard is legacy in the deep south, a next-generation *Andy Griffith Show* with car stunts and cute cousins in cutoff jeans. If Sunday sermons lacked practical application, one could always look to the Duke family for a lesson. The good life is one of friends and family. Trust God. Stay humble. Help everybody you can, even your enemies.

One day, while researching a project, I stumbled across John Schneider's IMDB page. That's the list of all the movies and TV shows a person has been in. Westerns, sci-fi, cartoons and prime-time soaps, John's show business resume was the longest I'd ever seen. And that didn't include his music career, a fistful of gold records and killer country songs.

One fact came as a shock. America's favorite redneck is from . . . a suburb of New York City. Wait, what? I wanted to hear that story. Why doesn't this guy have a book?

Hang on. I thought. *I work in the business of making books.*

I met Alicia and John in 2018 and we dove into the creation of his first memoir, from Manhattan to *Smokey & the Bandit,* the blessing and curse of being "Bo Duke." The storms of life had rained hellfire on John Schneider in the last few years. Divorce, bankruptcy, jail cells and floods. He'd sold off all his Dukes memorabilia, even the General Lee.

But then, he met Alicia Allain. She'd been through hell too, but they found each other, and in doing so, found a way to beat back the devil and move on. They were best friends, lovers, business partners, comedy team. It didn't take a writer with a psychology degree to see how much they adored each other.

I was sitting with them by a guitar-shaped pool in Music City when they first got news of her diagnosis. After all they'd been through, things were finally good. And now this? When Alicia excused herself to take a call, I turned to John.

"What are you going to do?" It wasn't just a writer question. I was concerned.

John didn't hesitate. "I'm going to marry her," he said. "And we're going to get through this the same way we've gotten through everything else in the last few years. Together."

John Schneider is not Bo Duke. But the character "Bo Duke" is 100% John. Fearless, reckless, respectful, always willing to stand up for what's right. And that's exactly what he did.

The three of us kept working as Alicia took charge and fought back with everything she had, never losing her humor and grit. I watched firsthand as her scans went from "lit up like a Christmas tree" to zero signs of activity in just a few months.

In 2020, when I experienced my own health crisis, Alicia and John were there with prayers, support and the reminder that I could not afford to be passive. God knows where I'd be if I had walked blindly into the jaws of the medical machine.

On a sunny spring day, we climbed Nashville's newest skyscraper to celebrate that we'd both come out on the other side, healthy and full of life. "We need to write a book about this," Alicia told me. "A lot of people are going through a hard time and they need help."

But then, everything went crazy again.

John

Shortly after Christmas, Alicia's kidneys crashed, her calcium levels skyrocketed and metastases started to flare up in other places. The pain was out of control and everything started to quickly spiral down.

It's the most difficult thing I've ever been through. It's too personal. It is still too hard.

Jamie

"Just rest," I told her. "We can work on the book later."

Alicia winced as the needle slipped into her vein, shifting in the recliner, trying to find a position that didn't hurt. "No," she groaned. "I need to do this now."

"But you're going through so much," I said. "One surgery after another, stiches and needles and procedures and scans and…."

We sat in silence as the IV dripped gold fluid through her veins. She nodded and reached to pat the back of my hand. "Maybe you're right."

When she said it, I noticed something in her eyes I'd never seen before. Not fear or fatigue or focusing on the next fire to put out. Something past all that. Something far away.

"What if it doesn't work?" I asked.

She laughed softly. "One way or another, I'm good."

Then Alicia did what she did best. She turned it around. "Come for Christmas," she said. "Bring your sweet wife. I'll fly you down."

"Aw, you don't have to do that."

"I want to. Y'all just come on."

"Alright," I replied. "Let me check. We'll finish your book then."

I stood to leave, one hand on the door. "Love you," she said. Alicia was never hesitant to say those words. It made me realize that I shouldn't be either. I should never miss a chance.

"Love you too, Ms. Alicia."

I drove home thinking about how strange and fragile this life can be. The only things that truly matter are God, good friends, family and the ability to laugh, even in the worst of times, because that's what faith is. The belief that one way or another, everything will be alright.

The next time I drove through the studio gates was for Alicia's Celebration of Life. I arrived the night before. John was sitting by the fire, staring into the flames. "I am so sorry," I said, holding out my hand.

John stood, grabbed my hand and threw his other arm around me. "This isn't how the book was supposed to end," he said.

We both broke, holding on to each other, not knowing what to say. Alicia's end goal was never to simply beat a disease. The goal was to be a conduit of grace, to laugh big and love hard, to enter the gates of Heaven and fall laughing into the arms of God. But the man she loved so fiercely was still here, hurting.

Finally, I said the only thing I could think of that was right. The only thing that matters after a person has fought the good fight.

"Don't worry, brother," I promised. "It won't."

Jessica

Growing up in Hollywood, I used to love driving through the hills with Mom in her little Porsche Boxter with the top down blaring Destiny's Child, both of us singing and laughing, hands up catching the warm California air.

She'd take me roller skating and I'd be embarrassed because she could skate so much better than me or my friends. Okay, embarrassed but also secretly *so* impressed.

After Mom's diagnosis in 2019, I began to spend more time at the studio property. When Mom and John were in town, I would come stay with them in the Roadhouse. Once the world shut down in 2020, I decided I would move down for a while. When I told Mom I wanted to move into the Blue Itsy cabin, her eyes lit up with joy. "Let's go to Target!" she said.

That woman bought me everything, from kitchenware to matching towels to cute pictures to hang on the wall. Then we went home and she called John over to help put it all in place. Yet again, she took charge, took care of me and - *poof * - made her vision come to life.

Mom was known for her strength, determination and drive, but behind her armor was a heart full of compassion, a mind of wisdom, pure grace pumping through her veins and a gentle touch. At her core was love.

Mom worked hard through difficult times, but when she was diagnosed with cancer it the first time she couldn't work herself out of a problem. She did a lot of things to gain control and studied cancer so she could fight it her way. But fighting required something different and that was a deeper faith in God.

After Mom's initial diagnosis, her faith began to blossom. She became more curious about what it meant to experience "Thy will be done on earth as it is in Heaven." On occasion she would take off her armor of strength and show her vulnerabilities, her fears and her heart. There was a deep element of trust that my mom had in God throughout her whole journey.

Mom fought with all she had and did it the only way she could: **her way**, by her own convictions, beliefs and faith in God to guide. If she hadn't, I don't think we would have been able to enjoy her for as long as we did.

Kim

God works in mysterious ways. We thought he sent Alicia to our clinic so we could help her. But really, God sent Alicia to teach and help us, to show us the beauty of life and appreciate the time we have on earth with those we love.

We could always feel Alicia and John's devotion, not only to each other, but also to battle a terminal illness as "the team to be reckoned with." Even in her most fragile moments, she was a brilliant, strong-willed warrior and a spitfire with the faith and courage to tackle each step of the unknown with a strength and humor that was truly one of a kind. Resilience and beauty radiated from Alicia and it was contagious. She made us all want to do better and be better. What a blessing!

Alicia was never okay just being a passenger on this journey. She was determined to be an advocate for others, trailblazing and sharing insights along the way. She spoke truth, bringing light and love to even the darkest of situations.

That kind of love will only multiply. That kind of light will never, ever go out. The next time we meet, she will be all faith and spitfire, a warrior who fought the good fight and changed lives in ways that we won't be able to comprehend until we get to Heaven. I can't wait!

Alfred Bonati

Twice in my life, I've been blessed with very special people who not only helped me to be a better person, but who also showed me the real path to heaven. One person was my wife and the other was Alicia Allain Schneider.

Whenever I see somebody suffering, I remember how Alicia handled this enormous mystery called pain with tremendous bravery, elegance, and kindness. We had amazing conversations about hope and trust, even as she faced the most difficult stage of her life. I never once heard her complain.

The love between John and Alicia was so evident and such an inspiration. They are very special to me and to the world. Even while fighting cancer, they took every opportunity to ask, "How can we help others going through this?" They did and I believe they will continue to do so.

Even as her time on earth grew short, Alicia was always thinking of others and looking towards the future. I miss my dear friend, but God kept her close and I know we will see each other again.

Lannie Guidry

In 1985, my parents moved from East Baton Rouge to a small suburb on the west side of town called Brusly. I'd been in Catholic school all my life and was never so nervous as the first day in a public high school. *Will the kids hate me? Am I going to have to eat lunch by myself?*

I was worrying about all those things when a beautiful, perky blonde bounced up to me in the hall. "Hey, what's your story?" she said. That girl was

Alicia. She had a gift for bringing people in and making them feel welcome all the way back in tenth grade.

Alicia was a cheerleader, so I tried out too. We had a lot of fun, made a lot of memories and made some trouble too, but we won't tell those stories here. Remember earlier in the book when she mentioned breaking her tailbone in a cheerleading accident? I was the one who dropped her that day. Acadian Ambulance had to come cart her off the field. She never let me live that one down.

You couldn't stop Alicia and before long, she was going again. She loved to dance even more than cheerleading and talked our principal into starting a dance line during our junior year. She even helped choreograph the routines. If Alicia set her mind to something....

The best times we had were in her little red Fiero with a license plate that said, "TOO CUTE." We'd cruise Railroad Avenue, music up, windows down, flirting, giggling, smoking cigarettes to look cool. What I wouldn't give to cruise Railroad with Alicia again.

When it came time for senior prom, the ruffles on my dress were so big that I couldn't even slow dance with my date. He just had to hold on to my elbows and sway. Big hair, big dresses. Everything was big in '87.

Alicia walked in and everybody's jaw hit the floor. She wore a tight green dress that showed off every curve of her tiny frame and instead of teasing her hair high and shellacking it with Aqua Net like the rest of us, hers was slicked back. That was Alicia. She always knew how to command a room, both beautiful and bad-ass, tough, but tender too. Alicia didn't follow trends. She made them. "Lannie, who cares what other people think?" she'd tell me. "As long as you're happy and it makes you feel good."

It was hard when Alicia moved to Los Angeles after high school, but we all knew Brusly was too small for someone with dreams as big as hers. We stayed in touch and a few years later, when she had a child, I was there. Raising Jessica as a single parent was difficult, but Alicia's biggest challenge was also her greatest triumph. She was so proud of Jessie. We all are.

When Alicia crossed paths with John Schneider, I knew she'd finally met her match, someone with the same drive and passion for life. John let Alicia be her true self without ever questioning why. She'd come up with some new idea to turn the world upside down and John would just smile and say, "Well, I don't see why not." Next thing you know, they'd make it happen.

When my father died in the ICU, John and Alicia were at the appointment where they confirmed her diagnosis. "Don't leave," she told me. "I'm coming for you."

We stood in the hospital parking lot and cried for the longest time, neither of us wanting to let go. So much devastating news that day. I lost my daddy and my best friend just found out she has cancer. It felt like such a long way from those two carefree teenagers we'd once been.

John's love for Alicia shone even brighter after she received news of her diagnosis. On their wedding day, when they said, "in sickness and in health," my throat clenched. Not everyone knew she was fighting cancer at that time.

That fight was a journey for Alicia, one that she took on with a mission to learn, teach and win. In my book, she did all of those things, immersing herself in research about foods, supplements and treatment without chemotherapy. John and Alicia visited doctors all over the country for advice and she never missed a chance to pass on what she'd learned, speaking to big groups and small, anywhere she could find to encourage or help someone along.

There were days when she was kicking cancer's ass, strutting in her heels, making things happen and it was like, "Huh, well, I'll be damn!" But there were hard days too, days when she would ask me to carry her cellphone because it was too heavy.

I've spent my career in the medical industry as a registered nurse and nurse practitioner. I saw all those scans she talks about in this book. The fact that she was walking was a miracle – but that's Alicia, the same fierce, strong girl I met nearly four decades ago.

I'd been at Alicia and John's house for several days since I was off of work. Alicia had fought so hard, but she was exhausted and her body was starting to shut down. We all gathered around, loving on her, laughing, telling stories from back in the day. God bless John, he was so tender and adoring. My heart was broken, but I was thankful they had found each other and he had taken such took good care of my friend.

It was Sunday, February 19th. There was a big Mardi Gras parade that night and my youngest son wanted me to come home and take him to the parade. "Go, your children miss you," Jessie told me. "Mom would want you to spend time with them."

Everybody cleared out of the room. It was just me and Alicia. I sat there for a while. Finally, Alicia's cousin, Joey, came in. "Did you give her permission to go yet?" she asked.

Even though she was suffering, even though she was so ready to see the Lord, I wasn't ready to let her go. Best friends for thirty-eight years. How do you let go?

"If you love her, you got to let her go, baby," Joey said softly. "Maybe she's waiting on you. Maybe she is waiting for you to say you're gonna be alright."

As Joey held my hand, I said goodbye. I drove home crying, thinking, praying. I believe with all my heart that I will see my friend again, that she's with Jesus and we will all be together in a place with no more pain or tears, where we'll never say goodbye again. But in that moment, my heart was so heavy and it just all hurt so bad.

I took my son to the Mardi Gras parade that night. The music was loud and people were dancing and having a good time. Even in all that pain, I couldn't help but smile and think, *my friend sure did love a good party.*

Alicia passed two days later, on Mardi Gras. Jessie and John were gracious enough to ask me to speak at her celebration of life. I don't know what your idea of Heaven is, but I believe it's going to be a good time. The best. I wouldn't be surprised, if on my first day there, I'll be walking the halls of Heaven and cross paths with a beautiful, perky blonde.

"Hey, girl," she'll say with that sneaky grin, "What's your story?"

And on that day, we will never let go again.

Jessica

Momma was my very best friend. We experienced many highs and lows together. That's just how it is between a single mom and her daughter. You become close in a different kind of way.

In a way, writing this feels like a lie. The fact that my mom is not physically here anymore is a reality I'm not ready to accept. I know she lives on through me and will live on through my kids and their children too. But those things will never replace having her here.

I was her caretaker to the end. It was an honor. It was also the hardest thing I have ever had to do. On one of her last days, she looked up at me and said, "I'm ready to go, Jessie."

"Where do you want to go, Momma?" I asked, thinking maybe she wanted to go home or to the beach.

"I'm ready to go be with Jesus. I have a new body there. New legs. I will see you on the other side. I love you. Everything I've ever done was because of you."

Then, in her final moments she told me she saw a bridge. Waiting on that bridge were her grandmother, Jesus and a brand-new young body, just for her. One with no cancer, no pain and no sadness.

Momma fought so hard for healing in this life. As I held her hand, she crossed that bridge. And in that moment, she was completely, totally, forever healed.

God never designed us to experience the pain of death or loss of a loved one. But there is hope. Evil doesn't win. Death has been defeated. My mom is dancing with Jesus in Heaven, full of joy and life.

Soon, we will be with her again.

John

Alicia Ann Allain Schneider was the bravest, most selfless person I have ever known. She endured her struggles with dignity and grace, the likes of which I have never seen. The kind of strength that can only come from God.

She fought that battle not only for herself, but also for you, working on this book, quite literally, until her last breath. Her sacrifice was not in vain. Alicia lived a life of victory to the very end, one that will help others long after I've sang my last song or jumped my last car.

Some might see her story as noble, but tragic. Alicia would never look at it that way. She had a pioneer spirit, ready and willing to go first and try something new. Great strides were made in the area of metastatic breast cancer that are a direct result of her courage and sacrifice. We have developed a theory of weakening cancer cells while strengthening the immune system that I believe will eventually become the new standard. Who knows, maybe they'll even call it "Alicia Therapy."

Remember when she told the doctor, "Do you know how long it's been since I could dance?"

I believe she is dancing and laughing in Heaven, right now, that everything I love about Alicia is more alive today than ever. And whether it's thirty days or thirty years away, she will meet me there, take my hand and with a smile say, "Hey, stranger. Did you miss me?"

We are still the team to beat, baby. Until that day . . .

THE TAKEAWAYS

"Let's talk about this in the abstract."
– Alicia Allain Schneider

Finishing this book was so hard, but it's been my hope and honor to share my Smile with you through these pages.

My sweet Smile and I did not get the victory we had hoped for, planned for, worked for and prayed so hard to get. But in no way does that diminish the victories we did share. Those victories can be yours too. Alicia wrote this book so that those who follow her path could have faith, strength and the belief that the ultimate victory can, should and will be yours.

"Baby," she would tell me, "If the road we're on doesn't go where we think it does, make damn sure it goes there for somebody else." Alicia lived to help others and there's no way that can ever be considered as anything but a win.

Still, this book began as a means to educate, inspire and guide those who are fighting a grim diagnosis or struggling to find their way through a very confusing medical system. So, what would we do differently? In closing, what lessons would we want to share?

First and foremost: Once you've made your cancer dog **SIT**, (I would define that as three clear PET scans in a row) your new mission is to figure out how to make it **STAY**.

If the side effects of your medication are too severe, then I suggest talking to your doctor about cutting them back by half or even two-thirds. If you're on Ibrance or Herceptin, maybe half your dose while still doing twenty-one days on and seven off.

If cancer has metastasized to the bone – even if you have clear PET scans – you might want to opt off of the bone density medication. I believe that much of Alicia's early bone pain was due to her medication. You should, however, continue to get a PET scan every six months if your insurance will allow it.

Most important, avoid any new hobbies that could break a bone or kill you! (a little humor is necessary for my soul these days.) Furthermore, if you are currently engaged in an activity like skydiving, rock climbing or racing cars, **stop**.

I will go to my grave believing that getting into a race car was a mistake. Cancer is a demon dog from hell that will take any opportunity to sink its teeth into you again. Most of Alicia's oncologists don't believe that's true, but her bone doctors agree, so you'll have to make up your own mind. Why risk it? As I used to say before racing, "There are very few golf fatalities…."

Regardless of the road you are on, **be the driver**. Stay in charge of your life for your own sanity and the sanity of those you love. If you're leading a passive life, can you really even call that living?

Lastly, don't let a day go by where you don't express your appreciation, admiration, respect and love for those God has put in your life. No matter how many days, months, years or decades you have with the one you love, it will never be enough.

So, beloved reader, do this: **Love one another.** Love one another as if this is your last day. Love one another as if this is *their* last day. But whatever you do, love one another.

Until that glorious day . . . be well,
Alicia & John Schneider

ACKNOWLEDGMENTS

We could not have made this book happen without Michael and Linda Allain, Daniel Turner, Jana Poche, Lannie Guidry, Mike Gursey, Tanya Mooney, Cody McCarver, Trevor Tyson, Joshua Bramlett, Vicky Lanzone, Carroll Moore, and Mindy Lloyd.

Special thanks to the staff at North Oaks Hospital, Gloria Willie, Megan Houghton, Kylie Roberson, Christine Massey, Cooper Watkins, Cassandra Williams, Courtney Dillard and Christy Heck who served our family faithfully in our most difficult time.

It would take another ten books to show appreciation to the people who helped us through these last few years. To all the fans and friends, old and new, who offered heartfelt prayers and words of encouragement – to everyone who ever put a smile on our faces.

We hope we put a smile on yours.

ONE LAST THING

Will you do us a favor? I've had a lot of success in my life, but I am now in a season of redefining victory. How do you define victory? How has that changed? What parts of this book spoke to you the most? I'd love to see what you come up with. Share it with us at **johnschneiderstudios.com** or www.facebook.com/johnschneiderstudios.

You do not walk this road alone. We are with you. God is with you. **Go Do**. Wherever you are called, to whatever God has called you to do. Somebody needs you. Make those you love proud.

This book is over, but the story has just begun . . .

CHAPTER ONE
LETTER TO HEAVEN

My beautiful Smile,

Thank you for showing up yesterday in what I can only describe as a
God-fueled, healing dream.

Heaven is real and closer than we think.

I will see you again…

I will hold you again…

We will be as we were here only much…

much…

better.

It's amazing how much you can hear when you remain silent.

I miss your touch…

Your humor…

Your grit…

Your grace.

I miss everything.

But I am one day closer to you.

Your loving husband,

Me

*I prayed to be helpful to others going through loss.

I have a feeling that a new adventure has just begun.

Made in the USA
Middletown, DE
17 November 2023

42887748R00076